GENGHIS KHAN

Conqueror
of the Medieval World

GENGHIS KHAN

Conqueror of the Medieval World

ROBERT N. WEBB

Franklin Watts, Inc.
575 Lexington Avenue
New York, N. Y., 10022

Cover photo courtesy of
The Bettman Archive
Map by Dyno Lowenstein

FIRST PRINTING
Copyright © 1967 by Franklin Watts, Inc.
Library of Congress Catalog Card Number: 67–16530
Printed in the United States of America

⅏⅏⅏⅏⅏⅏⅏⅏⅏⅏⅏⅏⅏⅏⅏⅏⅏⅏⅏⅏⅏⅏⅏⅏⅏⅏⅏⅏⅏

Contents

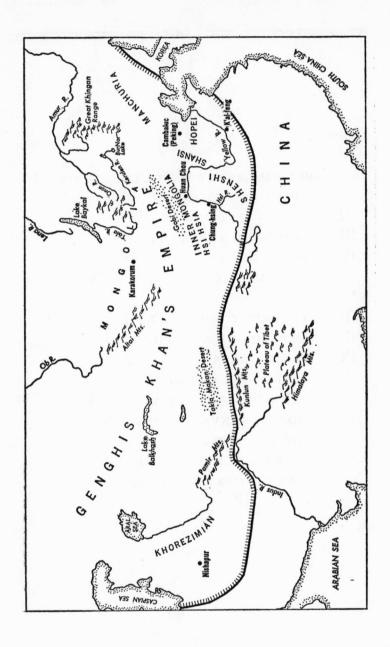

PROLOGUE:
The Great Mongol Conqueror

MANKIND has had many great conquerors in its history—Alexander the Great, Hannibal, Julius Caesar, Attila the Hun, Genghis Khan, Napoleon. Of them all, only the Mongol Genghis Khan died at the height of his power, the supreme master of the largest empire ever created in the lifetime of one man.

Unlike other conquerors, Genghis Khan never suffered a crushing defeat. Unlike other empire builders, whose empires crumbled with their deaths, Genghis Khan established a dynasty that ruled most of the world for nearly a century and a half after he died.

The conquests of Genghis Khan, his sons, and his grandsons—especially Kublai—gave the House of Khan an empire that stretched from the Sea of Japan deep into Western Europe. The territory ruled by the Mongols included all of China, India, Persia, Turkey, Russia, Poland, and Hungary. The rest of the European nations lived in constant fear that the Mongol hordes would

1

swoop down and add their lands to the holdings of the fierce warriors from the steppes of the Gobi Desert. Why the Mongol *Khans* (rulers) abandoned their conquest of all Europe has never been explained. Historians do not doubt that the Mongols could have extended their domination over the entire civilized world had they so desired.

China, India, and all of Asia are still referred to as "the mysterious East." But until the days of Genghis Khan, that vast area of towering mountains, burning deserts, slopes, and steppes, stretching thousands of miles in all directions, was virtually unknown to European civilization. Not until Subudei, one of Genghis Khan's greatest generals, easily captured Moscow and Kiev, extending Mongol dominance over all of Russia, did Europeans learn of the overwhelming power of the Mongol warriors.

Genghis Khan is the generally accepted spelling of the great Mongol's name. But his name also appears in reference works as Chingis, Chengis, Jenghis, and Jenghiz. When Genghis Khan was a thirteen-year-old boy called Temuchin, his conquering career began. In the year 1180, Temuchin's father died, and the young warrior became khan of a Mongol clan numbering just a few hundred families. At his death nearly fifty years later, Genghis Khan was the lord and master of millions upon millions of peoples of all races.

ONE

CHILD HORSEMAN AND HUNTER

TEMUCHIN was three years old. It was time that he learned to ride. His mother, Oelun Eke, strapped him firmly in the wooden saddle. She stepped back, slapped the horse on its broad rump, and sent it dashing across the treeless plain of the northern Gobi Desert.

Leather thongs, laced around the child's body and tied to the high front and back of the saddle, kept the boy from falling off. It was his first ride on a horse. He had ridden only on the back of a fat, woolly sheep, his strong, chubby hands clutching the deep, thick wool. But riding a horse was different—much different. Although Temuchin was tied in the saddle too tightly to fall off, controlling the horse with his small hands and arms was difficult. Horse and rider bounced across the plain. Temuchin struggled with the reins, and finally steered the horse back to the *ordu*, the tent village, of his clan.

By the time he was four, Temuchin rode with such

skill that it seemed as if he were part of his horse. It was then that he was given a bow and arrow. From break of day to fall of night the young Mongol rode and hunted. His skill with the bow and arrow became as superb as his skill in riding.

At the age of six, a proven hunter and horseman, his apprenticeship was behind him. Temuchin was allowed to hunt with his father, Yisugei, chieftain of the Kiyad clan of the Mongols. Time after time father and son rode out of the ordu. Often they would be away for three days, spending the entire time in the saddle. Their saddles became their homes. They ate in them. They slept in them. When the hunters returned with their kill—deer and bear when the hunting was good, fox, marten, or rats when the hunting was poor—the game went into a huge pot in the center of Yisugei's *yurt*. The yurt was a tent made of felt stretched over wattled poles, interwoven with branches and reeds. A small opening at the top let out the smoke of the cooking fire.

The yurt was the home of Temuchin, his three brothers, his two half brothers, his sister, his father, his mother, and his father's second wife. Often the tent was further crowded by the families of lesser clan chieftains who were visiting Yisugei.

When the game had been cooked, Yisugei's yurt filled up with other Kiyad warriors, those less fortunate in their continuing hunt for food. It was a rule that all food was shared by the clan.

4

The warriors always sat nearest the fire and received the first portions of the food. The women sat to the left of the men, with the old and feeble, and dug into what was left in the pot. The children, even Temuchin, whose father was the *baatur*, the head of the clan, stood on the fringe. They crowded into the yurt's small entrance and fought over the remaining scraps that were thrown to them. They even had to fight with the mongrel dogs for the bits of tough flesh and bone.

The daily life of the nomadic Mongol tribes roaming over vast stretches of the Gobi Desert in central Asia during the twelfth century was difficult, even in the good seasons. Children had to fend for themselves from the time they were weaned from their mothers' milk and switched to mare's milk. In the spring, food was plentiful. Cows gave milk; sheep fattened; game was abundant. In these short periods all the Mongols ate enormous amounts. They stuffed themselves, distending their stomachs with mutton and horseflesh, strengthening their bodies against the days of hunger that they knew would come.

In the winter, when the cold winds howled and snow covered the desert, the children went day after day with no food, or only scraps. When all the meat was gone, the Mongols survived on boiled millet (seed or grain). At times they ate a form of cheese called *kumiss*. It was made from milk that had been stored in leather pouches. When the milk had fermented, it was beaten into a greyish paste. This fermented cheese in a child's empty stomach turned the toddler into a staggerer.

But Temuchin would not always be hungry. The Kiyad clan would not always be forced to roam the Gobi Desert, moving from pasture to pasture, traveling south in the winters in their *kibitkas*, tent carts pulled along by slow-moving oxen. The day would come when Temuchin would be called the mighty manslayer, the perfect warrior, and the master of thrones and crowns.

He would conquer and rule half of the known world, a vast area which stretched from the China Sea to the banks of the Dnieper River in Russia and from the mountain peaks of Tibet to the shores of the Indian Ocean.

In 1190, when Temuchin was twenty-three, he was made ruler of many Mongol clans. Upon him was conferred the name that has come down through seven hundred years of history—Genghis Khan.

TWO

DRIVEN INTO HIDING

THE date of Genghis Khan's birth is variously given as 1155, 1162, and 1167, the last year being considered the most reliable.

Yisugei, the father, followed an age-old Mongol custom when naming his firstborn son. The baatur and his Kiyad warriors had been away from their ordu, warring against a tribe of Tatars. The tribe was defeated, and Temuchin, the Tatar leader, was captured. ("Tatar" was the Persian word for the Mongols. It became the more familiar "Tartar" after Tartarus, the word for hell in Greek mythology. The Persians believed that the Mongols were devils from hell.) When Yisugei returned home to the camp at Deliun-boldak—northwest of present-day Peking—his wife, Oelun Eke, greeted him with their firstborn child. The custom was to name an infant after some outstanding recent event in the clan's life. So Yisugei named his son Temuchin after the Tatar leader whom he had just captured.

7

Temuchin has two meanings. In Turko-Mongol, the name is spelled *Tumur-ji*, and means "the finest steel." The Chinese version of the name, *T'ie mou jen*, has a completely different meaning—"supreme earth man." Either meaning aptly fitted the youth who was to become Genghis Khan.

As a child, Temuchin had more duties than learning to ride and hunt. Like all Mongol boys, he had to fish the streams that the Mongols crossed as they trekked from winter grazing lands to summer grazing lands. The large herds of horses and cattle, driven ahead of the long string of kibitkas, were the charges of the boys, and it was their duty to round up strays and drive them back into the herds. Riding ahead of the main train of oxcarts which carried the yurts, the boys acted as sentinels, keeping their eyes on the skyline to watch for fast-striking raiders. Wars and raids were as much a part of the Mongols' daily life as riding and roaming.

For days on end Temuchin and the other boys kept to the saddle. Often they went without cooked food for several days at a time, and more often with no food at all.

As an eight-year-old, Temuchin was tall, taller than other boys his age. Since his neck was short, his head appeared to rest on his broad shoulders. His green eyes, which did not slant, shone out from beneath his sloping forehead. Long, reddish-brown hair fell in braids down his back to his waist. His skin was burned a deep yellow-brown from the winds and sun of the Gobi Desert.

8

Temuchin lay in waiting, concealed by low brush, near the place where he had buried the fish. He did not have long to wait. Soon he heard the slight noises made by someone making a stealthy approach, and Bekter came in sight, searching the ground around him carefully. Then he spotted the place where Temuchin had buried the fish. Bekter dug furiously into the ground. His dirt-stained hands seized the fish and tore off the leaves. He sunk his teeth into the raw flesh. Temuchin waited no longer. He sped back to the camp and told his brother Juchi Khassar what had happened.

The two boys cautiously made their way back to the spot where Bekter was gorging himself. There was little more than bones left of Temuchin's catch, the fish that was to have fed the whole family.

Temuchin and Juchi leaped on Bekter. Their knives flashed—and Bekter was dead. They had murdered their half brother.

The days went by—lean, hungry days. No one mentioned the disappearance of Bekter. The whole family sensed what had happpened, but no one wept over Bekter's absence—not his mother, his full brother, or his half brothers and half sister.

This horrible but necessary incident plunged the hungry family to even greater depths of despair. But as bad as things were, they would get worse.

Temuge Ochighin, Temuchin's youngest brother, had gone hunting. Late in the day he came rushing back into

When Temuchin was nine years old, he experienced great joy quickly followed by stark tragedy. He and his father were on one of their frequent food-hunting trips when nightfall found them far from their ordu. Father and son sought shelter for the night in the tent of a friendly warrior, Dai Sechen, chieftain of the Khongirad clan. Temuchin's eye was caught by the pretty face of six-year-old Burte, daughter of Dai Sechen.

Temuchin spoke to his father, telling him that he wanted the young girl for his wife. Yisugei in turn spoke to Dai Sechen, and the betrothal was arranged immediately. The next morning Yisugei departed, leaving his son behind in the yurt of Dai Sechen. This custom was common with the Mongols of that day. Temuchin was to spend several months with his future father-in-law. He would ride and hunt with him, and would become better acquainted with his betrothed before the wedding ceremony took place.

But Temuchin spent only a few days in Dai Sechen's yurt. Yisugei, on his way home, stopped to take food with a tribe of the conquered Tatars. When he resumed his journey, he was seized with terrifying stomach pains, and he realized that he had been poisoned. Spurring his horse to its greatest speed, Yisugei reached his yurt, staggered inside, and ordered his wife to send immediately for Temuchin.

The messenger dashed across the plain, and Temuchin was told of the poisoning. He mounted quickly, taking two spare horses with him. He lashed his steed to a dead run, changing horses when one tired. But by the time Temuchin rushed into his father's yurt, Yisugei was dead.

Although Yisugei had never taken the title of khan, he did control many other *omuk* (clans) and *yasun* (subclans). Now he was dead, and a nine-year-old boy stood in his place. The clans and sub-clans once ruled by the strong hand of Yisugei became restless. They scoffed at the thought of being ruled by young Temuchin.

When Yisugei's widow beseeched a clan chieftain to remain loyal to Temuchin, he replied, "The deepest wells are sometimes dry, and the hardest stone is sometimes broken. Why should we cling to thee? What have we to do with a woman and her children?"

For a few weeks, a handful of Kiyads did remain with Temuchin and Oelun Eke. But they, too, finally deserted. Temuchin, his mother, and the other children were abandoned and left to survive as best they could.

To be sure, Temuchin had the right to sit upon the white horse skin as khan of the Kiyad Mongols, but now his clan had deserted him. He knew that the struggle to live would be fierce. He knew, also, that enemies of the Kiyads would seize every opportunity to destroy Yisugei's son, now that the strong arm of the father was gone.

The open steppes of the Gobi Desert offered no protection from surprise attack. Therefore, the family fled, seeking refuge in the Burkhan Kahldun, the eastern spur of the Greater Khingan Mountains. There, for the next

few years, Temuchin, his mother, and family lived in hiding. Their only food fish, wild onions, garlic, and the roots It was a hard life, and only Oelun Ek minder that one day her sons would rega positions in the Mongol clans kept the

The Russian historian, B. Ya. Vladir *Life of Chingis-Khan,* wrote of this peri view of the pastoral nomad of the steppe ence was the most wretched imaginable.

Added to this wretchedness was the fact ber of the family was a thief. Temuchin an Juchi Khassar, Khachiun Ulchi, and Tem were little more than skin and bones, as w and his sister Taimulun. But his two half br to fare much better, particularly Bekter.

Temuchin could not believe that his Belgutai was the food thief, for he had shov to Temuchin on many occasions. There v thing for Temuchin to do. He must set a t the thief. Two days went by when no fish v no game was killed. The family survived on and garlic. Then Temuchin had a stroke caught a fine fish, large enough to make a s meal for the entire family. But Temuchin d his prize catch to his mother. Instead, he w fish in leaves, making sure that Bekter was wat and slipped away from the camp to hide the

the camp, fear showing in his eyes. As he had fruitlessly hunted, he had spotted members of the Taijiud clan in the area. They had been feudal foes of the Kiyads for many years. Targoutai, the chieftain, had long resented Yisugei's rule, and he had sworn on Yisugei's death that he himself would rule the Mongols. To do so he must kill Temuchin, the rightful khan by inheritance.

The family knew that it was being hunted, and that the hunters were closing in.

13

THREE

TEMUCHIN YOKED

THE horses were saddled instantly. The family worked in frantic haste, gathering up their few possessions and striking their yurt to flee even deeper into the hostile Greater Khingan Mountains.

But Targoutai and his warriors struck before the family could leave. Oelun Eke ordered Temuchin to mount his horse and try to escape. He was her firstborn; he was the rightful khan; his life must be saved. In the brief fight that took place, Temuchin and Juchi Khassar managed to make their escape. Targoutai spared the lives of the other members of the family, for he only wanted to capture and kill Temuchin.

Now the deadly hunt was on. Targoutai and a small band of Taijiuds took up the chase. Temuchin and Juchi could not be far ahead, and all Mongols could track a horse by instinct. Since the brothers had only one horse apiece, Temuchin's capture was inevitable so long as he could not find a fresh mount.

14

The two boys rode toward the mountains. At nightfall, hearing Targoutai and his men drawing closer, the brothers decided to separate. Temuchin would head deeper into the mountains. Juchi would lay back and try to draw the attackers off Temuchin's trail.

Temuchin was successful in his escape, but after several days in the higher mountains, the cold and lack of anything to eat forced him to attempt a desperate gamble. He had to make his way back through the Taijiuds, who, he knew, would be lying in wait for him. Leading his tired horse, Temuchin went back down the mountain. Although he was extremely cautious, the odds were too great against him. He was spotted, captured, and brought before Targoutai. The chieftain ordered Temuchin placed in a *kang*, a wooden yoke fastened tightly around the neck and resting on the shoulders. Temuchin's wrists were lashed to either end of the yoke, his arms outstretched to nearly their full length.

For days he remained fettered, and the Taijiuds moved back to their grazing grounds. In the ordu, Temuchin was thrown into a small yurt with a single guard to watch over him. The jubilant Targoutai led his warriors off to a feast to celebrate the capture of the young khan.

Temuchin knew what awaited him in the morning— torture and death. He much preferred death. The torture would bring on a slow death, as his body would be dismembered part by part.

The sounds of the feasting came clearly into the yurt,

15

and hours passed before the celebration was over. Then, as silence settled upon the ordu, the young prisoner looked closely at his guard. In the darkness of the yurt, Temuchin could barely make out the outline of the man. The guard was seated on the earth floor of the yurt. Temuchin noticed his head fall forward, then jerk erect.

Temuchin never took his eyes from the guard's body. Again and again the man's head dropped, only to snap back again. Then, at long last, his head dropped forward and remained slumped on his chest. Temuchin waited. He had to be certain that the guard was asleep. Finally, unable to hold himself back any longer, Temuchin crept stealthily forward. He stood over the man. His breathing seemed regular. He was fast asleep. Cautiously, Temuchin knelt in front of the guard, his wooden yoke level with the man's head. He would have one chance, and one chance only. He must knock him out with a single stroke. Temuchin twisted his shoulders. Then with all his strength, he swung the yoke in a deadly arc, striking the guard full in the head. The man slumped over.

Temuchin leaped to his feet and ran from the tent. In the faint light of a newly risen moon, he made for the dense brush north of the camp. Just beyond the heavier growth was the river he had crossed the day before. If he could recross it, he felt that he had a chance of getting to a small forest which lay beyond.

The going was rough. Time after time, Temuchin tripped and fell face down, hampered by the clumsy

16

yoke. Finally, as day was breaking, he reached the river bank. His face and body were bloodied from his many falls. He plunged into the refreshing waters of the river, and rested for the first time. He had had no sleep, and his body ached. As he sat in the shallow water at the river's edge, trying to soak up strength for his tired body, he heard shouts from behind him. His escape had been discovered, and once again the Taijiuds were after him.

Desperately, Temuchin looked around. There would be no chance to cross the river now, for he would be too easily spotted in midstream by the pursuing Taijiuds. But downstream, not too far away, he saw a bunch of willow rushes. He plunged into the river, letting the current drift him toward the rushes. Although he could not use his arms, he kicked powerfully to increase his speed.

At last he reached the welcoming rushes, and forced his way deeper and deeper into them. His pursuers had now reached the river. He heard shouted orders for the horsemen to spread out and search the riverbank.

Temuchin sank lower and lower into the river, the rushes closing over him. Only the wooden yoke and his head were above water. He tried but could not force his head under water against the buoyancy of the yoke. For hours Temuchin lay hidden in his watery hideout. Once he thought he had been spotted as a Taijiud plunged his horse into the rushes. The horse thrashed forward, coming to a stop only a few feet away. The search continued until late afternoon, but Temuchin remained in the rushes until long after nightfall. When he felt sure that the search had been abandoned, he crept back through the rushes to the main stream of the river. Slowly, kicking with his tired, numbed legs, he reached the opposite shore, and fell into an exhausted sleep.

The young Mongol awakened with a start. The sky was lightening in the east; soon it would be daylight. From across the river, he heard sounds that told him the Taijiuds were hunting him again. He had to get away. His young, tough body had regained much of its strength during his long, sound sleep, although his arms and shoulders still ached from the unnatural position in which they were held by the kang.

First, he must find a safe place to hide. Second, he must rid himself of the kang. Otherwise, he would starve to death. The last food he had eaten was the morning before, when one of his captors had crammed a small piece of dried meat into his mouth. Each day on the trek from the Greater Khingan Mountains back to the Taijiud's ordu, his food ration had been either a small piece of dried meat or a curd of kumiss. He had been given just enough to keep him alive until the Taijiuds could return to their home grazing grounds and celebrate before killing him.

Temuchin made his way deeper and deeper into the woods. The sounds from his pursuers grew fainter, and by midday he could no longer hear any noises behind him. He began to feel confident that he had shaken off his hunters. But he kept on, and did not stop until night-fall, when he found a small cave. Using his feet and the ends of the wooden yoke, Temuchin scratched up all the dead branches he could find. He pushed them into a pile in front of the cave's small opening. Then he crawled inside. With his feet, he pulled and pushed the dead branches in front of the cave's opening. It was the best he could do. If a Taijiud hunter noticed the cave entrance, despite his attempts to conceal it, Temuchin knew that he would be finished. The enemy would not allow him to escape a second time. Hungry and ex-hausted, he again fell into a deep sleep.

The next morning, he tried in every way to free himself from the kang. He sought out sharp-edged rocks and tried cutting the leather thongs which tightly bound his wrists to either end of the yoke. But it was no use. The leather thongs were too tough.

The yoke made it impossible for Temuchin to use his hands. He could not pull up any roots for what little nourishment there might be in them. There was only one course left—he would have to find help. Temuchin turned his tired, hungry body to the east, away from the Taijiuds, back toward the foothills of the Greater Khingan Moun-tains. A trail ran through these foothills. It was infre-quently used, but it was the only passage over the moun-tains into the plains.

At midmorning of the following day, Temuchin sat beside the trail, having reached it the night before. No one had come down the path since his arrival. Midday came, with the sun shining straight overhead, but still no sounds of anyone coming. By late afternoon, Temuchin's hopes were dim. Feeble, faint from hunger, he could hardly keep awake. His head dropped forward again and again, and he had to force himself to remain conscious. Several times he thought he heard someone coming down the path, but each time it turned out to be only his fevered imagination.

Temuchin stretched out on his stomach, his head pointing up the trail. Just at dusk, he thought he saw figures coming toward him, shadowy figures of men on horseback, or yurts moving atop oxcarts. He shook his head, forcing his eyes wide open. Would this once more be only a mirage, a dream conjured up by his wandering mind?

A small caravan drew closer. It was real! When the first horseman came near Temuchin, the youth staggered to his feet. He no longer cared, no longer thought about whether these wanderers were friend or foe.

The horse shied as Temuchin came to his feet, and the rider let out a howl of fear. The young Mongol presented a weird sight. Arms outstretched as if impaled on a cross, his clothing in shreds, his gaunt face streaked with blood, the young boy was a ghostly figure to frighten the bravest of men.

Temuchin staggered and fell. It was dark when he regained his senses. He found himself sitting against a

20

tree trunk, his wrists no longer bound. The kang had been split and had been removed from his shoulders. He stood up, and found his arms slowly rising from his sides, up to the outstretched position they had been bound in for so long. With great effort he forced them down. It was almost impossible for him to control their upward movement.

A short distance away, Temuchin saw the outlines of a yurt, lighted from within by a fire. The boy staggered and stumbled as he made his way to the tent. Inside, he found the family crouched around the cook pot. Temuchin's luck had changed. This was a friendly clan, one which had once been ruled by his father, but had drifted off when Yisugei died.

They welcomed the son of their former chieftain. They fed him and found him a place to sleep in their yurt. For days, as the tribe moved out of the mountains and onto the plains, Temuchin rode with them. He slept, concealed under cowhides, during the day. At night he would come out to exercise. He helped with the oxen and the horses. Slowly the boy regained his strength. By the middle of the second week, Temuchin was fully recovered.

Now he must find his family. He spoke to the clan chieftain and was given a horse.

Temuchin turned back to the Greater Khingan Mountains. His family might still be there, still hiding from the Taijiuds.

How long had it been since Temuchin and his family had been separated by Targoutai's raid? The boy had no idea of time. He could only judge by the change in seasons. Spring had been coming on when Targoutai struck. Now the days were growing shorter; fall was approaching. A full summer had passed since Temuchin and his brother had fled before their pursuers.

Several days later, Temuchin reached the former camp of his family. Weeds had grown over it, but under them he found traces of burnt hides, the remains of the family's yurt. He spent two days searching the surrounding area, but found no signs of his people. They must have returned to the plains during the summer. They would be safe, Temuchin knew, because he had not been with them. After all, it was he, Temuchin, whom enemies of the Kiyad clan wanted to destroy.

The boy headed back toward the plains. He was even more cautious now, and his cunning had increased. Weeks passed, and cold winter winds were sweeping the steppes before Temuchin found his family.

FOUR

TEMUCHIN TRIUMPHS

OELUN Eke had been near despair as she watched her sons Temuchin and Juchi Khassar ride off, closely followed by Targoutai. For one of the few times in her life, tears streaked down her face.

Later that night, when the Taijiud hunters returned, she was cheered to see that Temuchin had escaped. She stood firm and unmoving with the rest of her children huddled around her as the Taijiuds burned her yurt, destroyed her few but precious possessions, and rode off with the horses that she still had. The loss of these animals was the greatest blow of all, for horses were wealth to the nomadic Mongols. Once, less than a year before, Oelun Eke and Yisugei had owned hundreds of horses and had ruled clans that owned thousands more. Now, horseless, two of her sons gone, Oelun Eke's fortunes were at the lowest point in her life.

But this strong woman with her stubborn pride refused to give up. The following day, with her children

23

trailing behind her, Oelun Eke started down the mountain, heading back to the Onon River which split the steppes of the Gobi Desert. On the second day of their travel by foot, Juchi Khassar joined them.

Weeks later, footsore, hungry, and still bearing the sad weight of a missing son, Oelun Eke and her family reached the ordu where once her husband had ruled.

The fortunes of the family now changed for the better. A few families of the Kiyad clan repledged their allegiance to the wife of their former chieftain. Oelun Eke's strong will and even stronger urging brought more of the clan to her. She was determined that when Temuchin returned—and she felt sure he would—he would have some clansmen and some possessions to rule over.

Her hopes for Temuchin's return never faded, even as summer and fall went by and the cold winds from the mountains started to roar across the Gobi Desert.

Her hopes were rewarded with great joy when one day, late in the afternoon, Temuchin came riding across the plain and reined up in front of his mother's yurt. Feasting to celebrate the young khan's return took up the next several days. Those who came to the feast saw a great change in Temuchin. The young boy whom they had deserted had become a man. He was larger and stronger. He spoke little, but when he did speak, it was with wisdom and authority.

True, his family had only a small herd of cattle and only nine horses, but all guests and visitors saw in the young khan the strength and virtues that had been his father's. There was little doubt that one day he would be a leader, greater perhaps than even his father had been.

All went well for a time, and more and more families came to Temuchin's yurt, pledging themselves to the standard of the Kiyad clan, the standard of nine yak tails. Then, misfortune struck again.

Temuchin was awakened by his half brother Belgutai, who had been away hunting. He had come back empty-handed, but had even worse news. The horses had been stolen during the night. Of the nine that the family owned, only the horse that Belgutai had been riding remained.

A family council was held. They knew that the horses must have been stolen by a band of raiding Taijiuds. How better could they strike at Temuchin's growing power than by stealing his horses?

All the boys volunteered to go after the thieves, but Temuchin would have none of this. Only if he himself brought back the stolen horses could he repair the damage to his authority that had been inflicted by the theft.

Temuchin mounted the weary horse, ridden all the night before, and started after the Taijiuds. Once they had hunted him; now he was hunting them. He gave no thought to the fact that he was alone, that the odds against him would be great. He must get the horses back, or again the members of his clan would desert him.

Temuchin rode slowly at first, holding back his strong

desire to spur his horse to greater speed. He knew how tired the animal was. The loss of this horse would ruin any chance that he might have of regaining the stolen ones.

Tracking the Taijiuds and the horses was very easy for the young Mongol. When darkness came, boy and animal spent the chill night under the open skies. The next day the horse was rested, and they made better time. The tracks of the horse thieves were fresher.

On the third day of the hunt, Temuchin met a boy about his age, who was tending a small herd of horses. Temuchin asked the boy if he had seen a band of men driving eight horses along with them. The boy said that he had, late in the afternoon of the day before.

Temuchin and the stranger took an instant liking to each other. The boy's name was Bugurji, and he was a member of the Arulad clan of Mongols. Bugurji shared his food with Temuchin, and their liking for each other grew stronger. This was the beginning of a lifelong friendship. Bugurji remained with Temuchin and became one of his most outstanding generals.

The new friend offered to help Temuchin bring back the stolen animals. Temuchin accepted the offer without hesitation. Bugurji roped a horse from the herd he was tending, and Temuchin's tired horse was put to pasture with the others.

The two boys took up the pursuit. On the following

26

day they came in sight of the Taijiud camp. The eight stolen horses were grazing nearby. Bugurji looked at Temuchin, ready to follow his lead. Temuchin spurred his horse toward the camp, and Bugurji followed closely on his heels.

At a mad dead run, Temuchin cut between the camp and the grazing horses, driving the animals off. Bugurji, riding beside him, drove one side of the horses, Temuchin the other, keeping them in a tight herd.

The Taijiuds were momentarily stunned by this daring dash. But not for long. They mounted and galloped after the boys.

The eight horses were galloping at full speed, urged on by the shouts of the two boys. But the distance between them and the pursuers dwindled. Temuchin shouted at his new friend to keep up the drive. He slackened his speed, allowing Bugurji to go ahead.

The horseman leading the pursuit was drawing close to Temuchin. The boy took out an arrow and fixed it to his bow. Swirling in his saddle until the upper half of his body was facing backward, he let loose the arrow while his horse was at full gallop. The Taijiud fell from his saddle; the arrow had gone through his chest.

The other pursuing Taijiuds, amazed at the deadly accuracy of the bowman, reined in their horses, and stopped by their fallen comrade.

Temuchin spurred his horse and soon overtook Bugurji. Looking back, the two boys saw the other Taijiuds still huddled around the dead warrior. The enemy had given up the pursuit.

Five days later, Temuchin proudly rode back into the Kiyad ordu, driving the eight horses ahead of him.

FIVE

ACCLAIMED GENGHIS KHAN

BUGURJI, who had returned to his father's camp, rejoined Temuchin two days later. He found that his new friend was enjoying the praises of all in the ordu. Temuchin had also given full credit to the help he had received from Bugurji, for the young Mongol was always most generous to his friends, an outstanding feature that was to mark his life as Genghis Khan.

Most of the credit, however, went to Temuchin. As the months went by, he gained more and more adherents, and his clan increased. His authority became greater. He was truly becoming the khan, protector of the clan's families and herds.

Temuchin was nearing his seventeenth birthday. He decided that it was time to think of the girl who had been promised to him eight years before. He would now make Burte his wife. With Bugurji and Juchi Khassar riding with him, Temuchin rode to the camp of the Khonigirads, and presented himself to Dai Sechen, Burte's father.

29

Dai Sechen remained true to his pledge; Burte would become Temuchin's wife. Preparations began immediately for the ceremony. The Mongols did not often have an occasion for celebration, but when they did they made the most of it. The two events they celebrated most lavishly were weddings and burials. There was actually little difference between the two as far as celebration and gaiety went. These great feasts were called *ikhudurs,* and the ikhudur for the marriage of Temuchin and Burte would stretch out over four days.

One-string fiddles played for the celebrating Mongols. The warriors left their weapons in front of their yurts and gathered around, clapping their hands and drinking rice wine and fermented milk as fast as servants filled their cups. As the fiddlers' tempo increased, the warriors leaped to their feet to perform the dance of the wedding ceremony, staggering awkwardly in their clumsy deerskin boots.

Hundreds of pots were filled to the brim with herbs, roots, rice, and small pieces of game. On open fires, fattened lambs sizzled and spattered as they roasted. The eating, drinking, and dancing went on for three days.

On the fourth day, Burte waited in her father's yurt for the moment when the final act of the wedding would take place. She was dressed in a gown of white felt. Her long, heavy black hair hung in braids stuffed with silver coins. On her head she wore a huge pine cone decorated with silk. All was ready.

30

Outside the yurt, servants stood at the heads of several horses. Streamers of silk flowed to the ground from the cushioned saddles. The fourteen-year-old Burte ran from her father's yurt, followed by her sisters and handmaidens. They leaped into the saddles and dashed through the ordu.

Temuchin quickly followed. In mock struggles, he fought his way through Burte's sisters and handmaidens until his horse was racing alongside the animal bearing his bride. He swept her out of her saddle into his arms, and bore her off onto the plains. Temuchin had conquered and carried off his wife.

The next day Temuchin and his new wife rode back to his own ordu. Two servants rode beside Burte, one of them carrying a black sable cloak to be presented to Oelun Eke.

Burte was now the wife of a khan. She must watch over his yurt; milk his cows and horses; stand guard over his herds when Temuchin was away at war; make felt for the tents; sew his garments; and make his socks and sandals.

Temuchin's position and prestige were much improved by his marriage. More and more Kiyads came to swear allegiance to the standard of nine yak tails.

The young khan, always restless, was burning with ambition to reunite all members of the Kiyad clan and bring others under his rule. Now he took the first step toward his goal. With his constant companions Bugurji and his

31

brothers, Temuchin rode off to the valley of the Tola River, where the powerful Kerait clan made their camp. The Keraits were led by Tughrul Khan, an old friend of Temuchin's father. Although Tughrul ruled a powerful clan, he was not a great leader. Feared more than respected, he had become khan on his father's death by murdering two of his three uncles. The third uncle had escaped and had sought help from another clan, who gave him an army to overthrow Tughrul. The uncle was victorious, but Tughrul Khan was restored to leadership by help from Yisugei.

Temuchin was given a warm welcome and many gifts at the Kerait camp. In return, he presented the khan with a sable coat, the greatest and most symbolic gift one clan leader could present to another.

Not long after this visit, Temuchin was in great need of this renewed friendship. The Kiyads were growing in strength, but they were still the weakest of the many Mongol clans. Only a few weeks after Temuchin's return, a powerful band of barbaric Mergids rode out of the northern steppes and raided his ordu. They struck at night, hurling blazing torches at the felt yurts. The Kiyads fought back, with Temuchin leading his warriors on horseback.

The Kiyads finally drove off the raiders, but to Temuchin's great horror, the Mergids had captured Burte.

The young leader lost no time in seeking help from Tughrul Khan. A combined force of Kiyads and Keraits

took up the hunt. Months went by. Several times Temuchin's small army nearly caught up with the raiders,
but they always managed to escape. Finally the Mergids
were trapped along the banks of the Buura River. They
were cut down and totally defeated, and their surviving
warriors were slaughtered. Temuchin found Burte in a
cart-borne yurt.

Not long after their return to the Kiyad ordu, Burte
gave birth to a son, named Juchi, after Temuchin's
brother. Since Burte had spent many months as a prisoner of the Mergids, there was some doubt as to whether
Juchi was actually Temuchin's son. But the young khan
never questioned his son's paternity. He was as loyal to
Juchi as he was to the other sons Burte bore him—
Jaghatai, Ugedei, and Tului. Burte also remained his
principal wife, although he had many others. Throughout his life, Temuchin was served loyally and faithfully
by Burte, who more than once helped him by her sound
advice in situations that were filled with danger.

One such occasion came shortly after Temuchin had
brought Burte back to his ordu. In his expedition against
the Mergids, he had been thrown into close company
with a young Borjigin chieftain, Jamukha. Many years
before, Temuchin and Jamukha had become *anda*, blood
brothers, and the relationship had been reestablished in
the recent fighting. At the orders of Tughrul, Jamukha
also returned to Temuchin many clansmen who had deserted when Yisugei died. These additional clansmen-

33

warriors gave the young khan a much larger following.

The friendship between Temuchin and Jamukha lasted less than two years. Despite their being anda, Jamukha turned on Temuchin, and during the young khan's struggles became his most formidable enemy.

The historian Vladimirtsov tells of the first instance of Burte foreseeing a dangerous situation for her husband. The Kiyad clan was moving to summer grazing grounds, with Temuchin and Jamukha leading the migration. Jamukha turned to Temuchin and said, "Today if we camp on the hill-slope, those who tend the horses will get tents. If we camp by the stream, those who tend the sheep and lambs will get food." Puzzled by these words, Temuchin dropped back, waiting for his mother and Burte to ride up. Temuchin repeated Jamukha's words.

He waited for his mother's explanation, but Burte spoke first. "Of Jamukha, people say that he loves the new and despises the old; now he has had enough of us. Do not his words conceal some hostile intention against us? We must not stop; we must march on through the night. It is better to be parted from him."

Temuchin carefully considered his wife's interpretation. He believed her to be right and, instead of halting, he ordered his clan to march on through the night. In the morning, he found that men of the Jalai and Baarin clans had deserted Jamukha to join the standard of Temuchin. Again Temuchin's forces were increased, but Jamukha now became his sworn enemy.

The quarrel between these two men continued for years and was typical of the constant changing of allegiances by clansmen from one chieftain to another. Both Jamukha and Temuchin were subjects to some extent of their overlord, Tughrul Khan, head of the powerful Keraits. Both were of noble blood. In those days, clans and sub-clans would change their allegiance to whichever chieftain appeared to be the strongest. Hereditary prestige was strong, but clansmen looked for the leader who seemed most likely to protect them and improve their fortunes. Between Jamukha and Temuchin, the latter was demonstrating higher qualities of leadership and greater strength as a warrior.

News of the break between Temuchin and Jamukha spread rapidly throughout the Mongolian steppes. Leaders of the clans scattered across the desert saw in Temuchin a man destined for a great future, a man who could bring back to the Mongols their former power and glory.

In the year 1190, not long after the break between the two young chieftains, a great council of khans, called a *kurultai*, was assembled. The purpose was to choose a khan who would be recognized as the leader of all the Mongols. Some men at the kurultai had greater claims than had Temuchin to this exalted position. Among them was Altan Ochigin, son of the great Kutula Khan, who led the Mongols when they were united and all-powerful. When Kutula Khan was slain in battle, the Mongol decline in power began. Another was Kutchar, son of Yisugei's elder brother. A third was Sacha Biki, chief of the powerful Jurkin clan. It was Sacha Biki who announced the decision of the kuraltai to Temuchin.

"We have decided to proclaim thee khaghan. When you are khaghan we shall be in the front in every battle against your foes, and if we capture beautiful girls and women, we will give them to you. We will start earliest for the chase, and the animals we catch, we will give to you. If in battle we disobey your commands, or if in time of peace we do any injury to your interests, then you will take from us our wives and chattels, and leave us to our fate in the empty wilderness."

Temuchin took the oath and was proclaimed Temuchin Khaghan. He was given the name Genghis Khan.

Warriors pressed around to hear their new khan's reply.

"You that are assembled here, you parted with Jamukha and decided to join me. If the heaven preserves me and helps me, all of you, my old friends, will ultimately become my happy companions."

This account of how Temuchin became Genghis Khan is in *Yüan Ch'ao Pi Shih (The Secret or Official History of the Mongols)*.

Vladimirtsov has an explanation of the meaning of the name Genghis or Chingis, as he spells the conqueror's name. "It is only a plausible guess that it was the name of a spirit of light worshipped at that time by the Shamanist Mongols. The supposition is confirmed by the fact that many regarded Temuchin as predestined by the Sky."

Genghis Khan was now the acknowledged leader of many Mongol clans. Despite trials, dangers, and setbacks, he had risen to a position from which he could set out to conquer half the world. But many struggles still lay ahead. There would be fierce fighting among the clans he now ruled. His friend Tughrul Khan would turn on him time and time again. And Jamukha, embittered by the elevation of his blood brother to the supreme rule of the Mongols, would plot and fight to kill him.

There were others, too, among the widely scattered Mongol clans, who were to dispute the absolute rule of Genghis Khan, and many years were to pass in a succession of wars.

᠌᠌

SIX

ENDLESS WARS

TEMUCHIN became Genghis Khan at the age of twenty-three. He was young to hold such an exalted position, and now he had to prove that he deserved it; that he could weld the many, widely scattered, warring clans into a great and powerful Mongol empire.

The young Khan had one sworn enemy—Jamukha—and one sworn friend—Tughrul Khan. When Tughrul learned of Temuchin's election, he said, "It is very good that Genghis should have been made khaghan, for how indeed could you Mongols do without a khaghan? So mind that you do not undo what you have done by common consent."

Tughrul might well have listened to his own advice. In the next few years this vacillating ruler was to need and receive Genghis Khan's help. He was also to turn against Genghis on several occasions.

But the first to strike at the authority of the new Khan was Jamukha. Outwardly he swore his allegiance, but even as he did so he was plotting to attack Genghis. Supported by the Taijiuds, Jamukha and his clan made a surprise attack at Dalan Baljiut, near the source of the Onon River, where Genghis was resting his warriors following a border skirmish. Genghis was defeated and forced to retreat down the Onon.

Despite this defeat, coming so shortly after he had been elected, the new Khan's prestige and power became greater. Jamukha's cruelty contributed to this strange turn of events. In defeating Genghis, Jamukha had captured seventy nobles and had boiled them alive in oil. This brutal act caused many of his followers to desert him and join Genghis as he retreated down the Onon. Among these deserters were the Uruds, a powerful Mongol clan numbering four thousand warriors. Others who joined Genghis were the Manguds and the Khongkhotats, the latter ruled by a chieftain named Munglik, an old friend of Genghis' father. In gratitude to Munglik for adding his men to Genghis' forces, Genghis gave his mother to the chieftain as a bride. He also made an alliance with the chief of the Khorolas by giving him his sister, Taimulun.

The first of several ironic twists in Genghis' relations with Tughrul came when Tughrul was defeated by his brother Erke Khara, and driven from his throne. For several months the deposed leader roamed the desert, seeking help but always being turned down. Finally he returned and sought help from Genghis. The positions of the two were now completely reversed. Genghis was the strong Khan; Tughrul was helpless. But Yisugei before him had aided Tughrul, and so Genghis did the same. He still paid respect to Tughrul as his onetime overlord. Taking up arms again, he defeated Erke Khara and restored Tughrul to power. This act brought further prestige to the Mongol Khan. Other clan chieftains admired his generosity, and Genghis Khan gained additional stature as a strong leader. Genghis also rescued Tughrul's brother Djagambo from the Chinese.

In 1197, Genghis Khan again saved Tughrul from being driven from his throne. Genghis had learned of a plot by Tutka Biki, chief of the Mergids, whom Genghis had never forgiven for stealing his wife. Tutka Biki, feeling that Tughrul Khan was still weak and his clan still divided in their loyalty, moved down the valley of the Mandja to attack Tughrul. Genghis cut them off in a surprise attack and defeated the Mergids. Then he went even further. All the booty captured from the Mergids was sent to Tughrul.

A year later, Tughrul had an opportunity to return this gesture, but failed to do so. Greatly strengthened since the defeat of the Mergids, Tughrul decided to attack them himself, which he did succecssfully. In the battle, Tutka Biki was driven far from his grazing lands, his eldest son was slain, and two others were captured. Much booty was taken—warriors, women, cattle, and horses. Tughrul kept everything for himself, sending not one part of it to Genghis, who was bitter about Tughrul's ingratitude but said nothing. However, this behavior did not go unnoticed by the other Mongol chiefs. Again Genghis' prestige was enhanced because he had held back when, by all rights, he could have punished Tughrul.

In 1198, Genghis and Tughrul joined forces with the Chinese to put down an uprising by the Tatars. Before entering into this brief war, Genghis had sought aid from the Jurkins, but their chiefs, Sacha Biki and Taichu, refused to join him. They had been among the most outspoken in favor of Genghis at the council when he was elected Khan. But now, realizing that Genghis meant to rule as he was elected to do, they decided to secede. When Genghis returned from his expedition, he captured the two Jurkin chiefs and executed them.

Shortly after, Tughrul openly betrayed Genghis, and Jamukha played an important part in this betrayal. Once again Genghis' Kiyads and Tughrul's Keraits were on the warpath. Inanch Bilkha, head of the powerful Naiman nation had died. In dividing his clan, his two sons, Bai Bukha and Buyuruk, quarreled over possession of one of their father's concubines, and a civil war broke out. Genghis and Tughrul decided to take advantage of this quarrel to crush the Naimans. Although Jamukha was Genghis Khan's open enemy, he marched with them. He was still a vassal of Tughrul.

The combined forces made short work of defeating Buyuruk. His brother, now alarmed, dispatched an army

41

under Koksu Sabrak, his chief general, to challenge the advance of the Keraits. A fierce battle began at daybreak and continued until nightfall, with neither side gaining victory. When darkness brought the conflict to a halt, Jamukha made his move to destroy Genghis Khan. He went to Tughrul and blamed Genghis for the failure to achieve victory. He convinced the elder khan that Genghis planned to join the Naimans. Tughrul left his camp-fires burning brightly to trick Genghis, and ordered his men to retreat. Genghis now had only his much smaller 'force of Kiyads to face the enemy.

At dawn the next day, Genghis saw what had happened. He knew that he could not possibly stand up against the stronger Naimans and he ordered a retreat. He was able to get away before the enemy could renew its attack, and he marched back toward the Kiyad grazing lands. His retreat was remarkable, for he brought his army back intact.

However, fate was not as kind to Tughrul. He was hotly pursued by the Naimans under General Koksu Sabrak, who caught up with the rear guard and crushed it. Continuing to press after the main body, Sabrak routed the Keraits, captured all their baggage and many horses, and forced them into disordered flight. Ilkha, Tughrul's son and heir apparent, rallied as many of his warriors as he could and checked the Naiman advance.

Now desperate, Tughrul dispatched messengers to Genghis Khan, pleading for help. Although Tughrul was in this situation because he had betrayed Genghis, the Mongol leader realized that the defeat of the Keraits would seriously endanger his own safety and position. Therefore, he decided to help his betrayer. He sent out a force under his four best commanders, Bugurji, Mukhali, Jelmei, and Chilaun. They came to Ilkha's rescue just as he was on the brink of defeat and smashed the Naimans, forcing them to return all the booty that they had plundered.

But there was still no peace for Genghis Khan. Now Tutka Biki, whom Genghis had defeated less than a year before, took up arms against him again. He attacked with a combined force of Mergids and Taijiuds. Tutka Biki suffered a serious defeat and was driven into hiding.

The power of Genghis Khan was rising, so, in 1200, other clan leaders decided that they must join forces and defeat Genghis before he overwhelmed them. Five clans joined together for the attempt. They were the Taijiuds, rallied from their hiding places, the Khatakins, Saljiuds, Durbens, and Khonigirads. However, their plans were revealed to Genghis by his father-in-law, Dai Sechen. This time, with no help from Tughrul, Genghis attacked before the five clans had fully united, smashed the Taijiuds and Durbens on the Bur Nor (a lake), then swung into action against the Khatakins, Saljiuds, and Khonigirads at another lake, the Kulum Nor, and sent them all down in defeat.

Although defeated time and again by Genghis Khan,

43

jealous clan leaders refused to give up. Jamukha, for one, still had dreams of replacing his blood brother. Under his leadership, an even more formidable force of warriors was gathered in 1201. Now arrayed against Genghis Khan were Jamukha's clan, and the five clans which had opposed Genghis the year before. In addition to these, the Ikiras and the Khorolas joined in. With such powerful backing, Jamukha was also able to induce contingents from the Mergids, Oirads, Tatars, and Naimans.

Loyalties meant nothing. Genghis' own father-in-law was head of the Khonigirads, but he was unable to control sub-clan leaders under him. The Khorolas also fought against Genghis, yet his own sister was married to Podu, the chieftain.

Genghis Khan knew that he could not hope to conquer such a large enemy force, and he called on Tughrul for help. Again Jamukha's plans had been betrayed to Genghis. With Tughrul, Genghis rode swiftly down the Kerulen River and surprised Jamukha's larger force on a plain between the Bur Nor and Kulun Nor lakes. The battle was brief but decisive. Genghis and Tughrul split the ranks of the clan confederacy and scattered them widely, and the coalition army was defeated.

With such success against a combined force much larger than his own, Genghis decided that he could strike against the Mongols' old enemy, the Tatars. It is a testament to Genghis Khan's great physical strength that he carried on war after war with little or no rest in between.

In the spring of 1202, Genghis marched east and met the Tatars in an important battle. On the eve of the contest, according to Vladimirtsov, Genghis called his officers before him and issued the following order of battle for the next day.

"If we are victorious, you shall not seek for booty; when it is all over it will be divided into equal shares. If the soldiers are forced to fall back to the initial position, they shall advance again and fight with increased vigor. He who, having retreated, does not resume the advance, will be beheaded."

The battle was a rout, and the Tatars completely overwhelmed. During its early stages, Genghis' uncle Daaritai, and two other noblemen, Altan and Kuchar, disobeyed Genghis' order. They began looting the enemy, keeping the spoils for themselves. Genghis Khan wasted no time in showing that his orders were to be obeyed to the letter. He had the three noblemen brought before him. He took from them all the booty that they had plundered, divided it among the others, and left the three looters with no spoils from the battle.

By this action Genghis earned the secret enmity of the three men, but he strengthened his own position with other officers and men by showing that regardless of rank or noble blood, he was fair in his dealings with his warriors.

Following the battle, a hot pursuit of the enemy brought almost all the Tatars into Genghis' camp as prisoners. Ruthlessly, Genghis ordered the slaughter of every male Tatar who stood higher than the hub of a cart wheel. The children and women were spared and were divided among Genghis' subjects as servants. Genghis took two Tatar women, Yesui and Yesugan, as his wives.

Riding high with his success over his longtime enemy, Genghis found that the greater his power, the greater the envy of those who wanted to wrest it from him.

He knew the time had come when he must stand alone. No longer could he depend on allies. His first step would have to be the conquest and complete domination of the Keraits, once his strongest ally. He would also have to eliminate Tughrul Khan. He could no longer put up with his changing loyalties. Throughout his lifetime, Genghis Khan's foremost belief was in the necessity of loyalty. To those loyal to him, he was always generous and fair. To the disloyal, he was ruthless.

SEVEN

TUGHRUL'S DOWNFALL

THE breach between Genghis Khan and Tughrul was widened by an incident which was of no great importance, but which infuriated the Mongol Khan. It led to treachery followed by more treachery.

Genghis' first plan was to cement relations with the Keraits by a friendly gesture. He asked Tughrul for a Kerait princess to become the wife of his son Juchi. In return, he offered one of his own daughters as a bride for one of Tughrul's grandsons.

But Tughrul disdainfully refused the offer. The rejection, according to the *Yüan Ch'ao Pi Shih*, "chilled the heart of Genghis Khan."

Jamukha, always ready to seize an opportunity to cause enmity and distrust between the old Khan and the young Khan, used this occasion to make another move against Genghis. He had already convinced Ilkha, Tughrul's son, that Genghis must be destroyed. Now he once more persuaded the old man that Genghis was plotting with the Naimans behind Tughrul's back.

Jamukha also played on the pride of the three noblemen whom Genghis had humiliated by stripping them of their booty when they had disobeyed his battle orders. These three leaders pulled their clansmen away. They had large followings, and their defection left Genghis' forces greatly reduced in strength.

Jamukha tried to get Tughrul to attack Genghis at once. The Keraits were greater in strength than the Kiyads, and they had been further strengthened by the deserters. But Tughrul held back. He had too much respect for Genghis' military strategy to feel that he could win an easy victory. Instead, he decided to use treachery to gain his ends. He sent a message to Genghis, saying that he had changed his mind. Now he was willing, even eager, to go through with the marriage proposals he had so recently rejected. He asked that Genghis come in person to discuss arrangements for the wedding ceremonies. But this last suggestion aroused Genghis' suspicions. It was a good thing he was wary, for his spies found out that Tughrul wanted to get Genghis into his camp to kill him.

Since treachery failed to work, Tughrul decided to attack. The onetime allies met near the Khingan Mountains and fought savagely throughout the day. Darkness brought a stop to the fighting with neither side gaining an advantage. Genghis took stock of the situation. It was bad. Since he was outnumbered three to one by the Kerait forces, he decided to abandon the struggle and withdraw his troops during the night. Tughrul failed to pursue Genghis, a decision which proved fatal. Perhaps he decided to give up the pursuit because Ilkha had been seriously wounded in the battle the day before. Whatever convinced him to make this decision, it led to his ultimate downfall.

Genghis Khan, his army reduced to four thousand men by death in battle or desertion, retreated to the forests of the Khingan Mountains. After his warriors and horses had rested, he led his army back to the Kulum Nor, where he made permanent camp. While there, he was joined by the Khonigirads, adding a few hundred warriors to his forces.

What Genghis Khan needed most of all now was time. He must increase the size of his following if he was to defeat Tughrul and gain control of the Keraits. He prepared a long message to Tughrul offering to renew their old friendship. The following text of this message comes in part from the French historian Fernand Grenard's *Genghis-Khan,* with certain changes made by H. Desmond Martin, author of *The Rise of Chinghis Khan and His Conquest of North China.*

Oh Khan my lord, have you forgotten the days when, driven from your throne, my father came to your help, overthrew the usurper and swore to be your brother? Is it not for that that I call you father?

Again, Oh Khan my father, was it not at my call that your brother returned from his flight into distant lands? Did I not save him from the ambuscades of the Mergids?

Again, Oh Khan my father, you came before me as a smouldering fire and as the sun behind the clouds; I gave you food and clothed you with garments. I took from the enemy [the Mergids] their herds, their tents—even their clothing—and all of it gave to you as a gift. When I saw you exhausted, haggard, and faint, I did not allow you to suffer hunger one day. I have not left you destitute a single month.

When I sent my spies among the Mergids, you took opportunity to go against them without waiting for me. You captured from their chief his children, his wives, and made prisoner a whole clan without giving me a soul. Nevertheless later when the Naimans surprised you so that you lost your people, your goods and fled, I sent to you my four heroes, Bugurji, Chilaun, Borokul, and Mukhali; they restored to you your possessions without recompense.

Again, like a gerfalcon, I crossed the Bur Nor and took for you the cranes with the azure feet, who are the Durbens and the Taijiuds, from there, passing as a falcon to the Kulun Nor, I took for you the blue cranes with the blue feet, who are the Khatakins, Khonigirads and Saljiuds.

Also, have we not made a pact to protect ourselves against calumny? When a venemous serpent would distill envy and suspicion in us, we ought to consult together and dispell all error, to believe nothing in advance and to keep our hearts unchanged. But, when a false statement was made against me, you believed it, you allowed it to undermine your faith. Without searching after the truth, you upheld yourself on it in order to separate from your faithful son.

Finally, Oh Khan my father, I have right on my side. What have I done to frighten you? Why are you unable to remain calm and without fear? I, your son, have I complained that I have been ill treated? That my lot was hard; that I wished better? When one of the wheels of a wagon is broken, it is unable to advance and if the ox pulls beyond its strength, it galls its neck and its efforts are in vain. If one unyokes it and leaves the cart alone in the road, brigands on the watch come and take all, and if the ox is left yoked it will die of hunger. This cart, my father, resembles us. We are two wheels which can only turn together.

At the same time, Genghis Khan sent messages to those relatives who had betrayed him. Again according to Grenard, the messages stated:

You conspire after my death. However, from the first day, I said why is it that the sacred country of our ancestors is always without a lord or master? To you Kuchar, I said: Son of Taiji, be Khan. You refused. I said to you Altan, son of Kutula Khan, who was once our chief, be in turn as your father our Khan. You were unwilling and I was greatly afflicted. At your instigation, I ascended the throne. You declared, it is you who will be Khan. I consented and said: I will not leave our country to dwindle away. I will guard intact its laws and usages. Of your own free will, you elected me in order to prevent outsiders from taking the sacred mountain where the three rivers rise. As chief of numerous people and commander of the army, I have given to all the accustomed gifts. I have captured great herds, women, youth, tents without number, and have made presents of everything. I have driven toward you the game of the mountains, I have beaten up the game of the plains. Now you follow my father the Khan; doubtless you know that he is broken and unstable. One pities me now. Wait until next winter and be not surprised if then people pity you.

Genghis Khan's indictment of Tughrul and his recalling of past pledges accomplished nothing. There could be no peace. But he did gain the time he so sorely needed, and his following increased. Many came over from the

Keraits because they were beginning to doubt the strength of their own leader.

When Genghis Khan's following had grown to the point at which he felt strong enough to attack, the Mongol himself resorted to treachery. He sent a message to Tughrul asking that the family of his brother Juchi, held captive by Tughrul, be released.

Tughrul sent two men to negotiate the family's return. They told Genghis that Tughrul and his Keraits were resting, feasting, and unprepared for battle. The Mongol acted swiftly, striking at Tughrul near the headwaters of the Jedjer Undur River. Despite the surprise of Genghis' swift attack, the Keraits defended themselves with furious fighting for three days before they surrendered. Among the few to escape were Tughrul Khan and his son Ilkha. They sought refuge in the Naiman clan of Bai Bukha, which had once defeated them.

Tughrul either was not recognized by the Naimans or was perhaps still regarded as an enemy, because he was slain by Khorisu Bechi, the Naimans' chief general. When his head was brought to Bai Bukha, the chieftain wept over the death of his former enemy. He had Tughrul's skull lined with silver and made into a cup, which remained an object of veneration in Bai Bukha's tent.

Ilkha continued his flight, making his way westward. In the Uighur kingdom of the T'ien Shan, he became an officer in a Turkish army. Much later he was captured and killed.

The vanquished Keraits were divided among the Mongol clans, and the noblemen made vassals of Genghis Khan. One of them, Khaduk Baatur, was to become an outstanding figure in the Mongolian empire. When Baatur was brought before Genghis after the defeat, the Mongol asked him why he had held out and fought so stubbornly when he knew that all was lost. The Kerait warrior, according to Vladimirtsov, replied, "It would have been unbearable for me to allow you to take and kill my lawful lord; I fought three days to give Tughrul Khan time to escape as far as possible. Now if you bid me die, I will die; if you grant me live, I will serve you with zeal."

Genghis' reply demonstrated how much he admired loyalty.

"One who refused to abandon his lord, and in order that the latter might win time and space, fought single-handed against me for three days, is a gallant man. Be you my companion."

By his victory over the Keraits, Genghis Khan had become the most powerful leader of the steppes of Northern Mongolia. But he still had many strong enemies. One of these was Bai Bukha, the Naiman chieftain.

EIGHT

EMPEROR OF MONGOLIA

THE expansion of Genghis Khan's power over the nations on the steppes of the Gobi drove Bai Bukha to made one more attempt to destroy the Mongol Khan. As the T'ai-yang (ruler), Bukha was the reigning head of the area north of the Gobi Desert. His vast grazing lands were in the northwestern part of Mongolia, near the Altai Mountains.

Bai Bukha knew that he would be attacked, since only he remained a challenger to Genghis Khan's desire to become emperor of all Mongolia. The Naiman chief decided to act quickly and rally around him enough forces to turn back the attackers.

For the fourth time, enemies of Genghis were called to form a coalition against him. Bai Bukha first enlisted the support of Genghis' longtime enemy, Jamukha, and the Jajirads. During the winter of 1203–04, Jamukha rallied to his standard the Durben, Khatakin, and Saljiud clans, a few clans of Tatars, those Keraits who had escaped, the Oirads, and the Mergids. These same clans had fought Genghis on many previous occasions and had been defeated. Desperate now, they were willing to challenge the mighty Genghis once more.

To further strengthen his position, Bai Bukha sought help from the powerful Ongud clan, asking the leader, Alakush Tagin, to attack Genghis from the south. According to the *Yüan Sheng Wu Ch'in Cheng Lu*, another history of the Mongols, Bai Bukha's message to Alakush Tagin read, "You know that the sun and the moon reign in the heavens together, but on earth there cannot be two rulers: be my right wing and we will take from Chingis Khan his bow and his arrows."

But Alakush had too much respect for the bow and the arrows of Genghis, and he refused. He went even further. He sent word to Genghis of Bai Bukha's request, and stated that he and his warriors would march north to help Genghis. So pleased was the Khan by this offer to help that he sent Alakush Tagin five hundred horses and one thousand sheep.

The march westward toward the Naiman Empire began when the snows still covered the plateau near the mouth of the Kerulen River, where Genghis Khan's warriors were gathered. By early summer, the Mongol army had marched seven hundred miles to the border of the Naiman country. Genghis Khan called a halt and rested his men and horses until autumn.

When the westward march was resumed, the forward

scouts of the Mongols first made contact with Naiman sentinels watching from the Khan Kharka Mountains.

On the slopes of the mountains, before Mount Naku, Bai Bukha's forces totaled fifty-five thousand men. Genghis Khan's army was smaller, numbering about forty-five thousand. These were the two greatest, most powerful armies ever assembled in Mongolia. They faced one another for the fierce battle that would decide who would rule.

Before ordering his men into battle, Genghis called a council of his officers, and strategy was discussed. It was decided that before the attack, the Mongol Khan's weary warriors and horses should be rested. To fool the enemy and conceal the actual number of his forces, Genghis ordered each of his soldiers to build five fires. The strategy worked. The historian Mouradgea D'Ohsson states that Bai Bukha thought Genghis' army was much larger than his spies had reported.

"One thought that the Mongol cavalry was foundered, but they have more camp fires than there are stars in the sky. The battle will be terrible. They are warriors who throw themselves in combat without blinking an eye; even when wounded in the face so that blood streams down, they never falter. Is it wise to seek battle with them here? Surely it is better to retire behind the Altai. Our horses are in good condition. Following us, the enemy will become exhausted and then we can fall upon them."

Bai Bukha was not known for his bravery. In fact, he

had never led his warriors into battle. His alarm at meeting the enemy brought scornful words from his son, Kuchluk. "The T'ai-yang trembles like a woman," he said to his father. "What of the numbers of the Mongols? The greater part of them have passed over to us with Mamuuka. But my father has never made a campaign. He has never been further from home than a calf goes to pasture."

Angered at his son, Bai Bukha replied, "Kuchluk is a young man of abounding conceit; let us hope that in the hour of battle, when death hovers over him, this dauntless courage does not vanish."

The officers of the Naiman army sided with Kuchluk. Khorisu Bechi, the chief general, spoke scornfully to his chieftain. "On the day of battle, your father Inanch Bilkha never showed the backs of his soldiers nor the cruppers of their horses to the enemy. But you, are you already afraid? If we had known you to be so fearful, we would have preferred to give command of the army to Princess Gurbesu, although she is but a woman. For you, faint-hearted T'ai-yang, it is here that you would hide yourself."

These words were too much for Bai Bukha. Furious, he ordered his army to move out. They marched for Chakirmaut, at the foot of Mount Naku.

Genghis Khan watched the downward movement of the Naiman warriors. He assigned Juchi Khassar to command the center of his army. The rear guard was placed in command of Temuge Ochigin. The vanguard, the forward troops, were led by Jelmei, Kublai, Jebe, and Subudei. The Manguds and the Uruds, Genghis Khan's crack troops, were stationed on the left and right wings. Genghis led a body of select troops, swinging along the line of battle to strike wherever the Naimans seemed to be gaining an advantage.

This great battle, considered by many historians the most important in Genghis Khan's career, is described in the *Yüan Ch'ao Pi Shih* (*The Secret or Official History of the Mongols*) in a dialogue between Bai Bukha and Jamukha. As the vanguard drove the Naimans back, Bai Bukha asked, "Who are those that pursue our men in the manner of wolves pursuing a flock of sheep to their very pens?"

Jamukha replied, "They are the four hounds of Temuchin fed on human flesh; he keeps them leashed on an iron chain; their skulls are of brass, their teeth like chisels; their tongues are like bodkins, their hearts of iron. Instead of horse whips, they carry curved swords. They drink dew; they ride with the wind; in battle they devour human flesh. Now they have been unleashed; their spittle runs; they are full of joy. These hounds are Jebe, Kubilai, Jelmei, and Subudei."

The fearful Bai Bukha was even more frightened. He ordered his troops to withdraw to the foothills of Mount Naku. The Mongols stepped up their pursuit, riding in among the retreating Naimans and slashing them down.

The Manguds and Uruds closed in from the right and left flanks. Bai Bukha turned again to Jamukha.

"And who are those warriors, like young horses loosened at daybreak, gorged with mare's milk and gamboling about their mother, who hurl themselves forward to outflank us?"

"They are the soldiers of the Uruds and Manguds," Jamukha answered. "They pursue armed men like game, they tear from them their blood-stained weapons, they slay them and take from them everything."

A retreat farther up the mountain was ordered.

"Who is that behind them like a hungry falcon impatient to advance?" the T'ai-yang asked.

"That is my sworn brother Temuchin, clad from head to foot in iron armor; he has flown hither like a hungry vulture; do you see him? You used to say that as soon as the Mongol comes he will fare like the lamb and not even his hoofs or hide will remain. But behold!"

As the Naimans were driven farther and farther up the mountain, Bai Bukha spoke again. "Who is that other chief that advances against us?"

"That," said Jamukha, "is one of the sons of Oelun, fed on human flesh. He is over eighteen feet tall. At a single meal he devours a sheep of three years. He wears a triple cuirass [armor]; he is more powerful than three bulls. He can swallow a man entire with his quiver without choking or even losing his appetite. When the fury of battle comes over him and he looses his irresistible arrows, he transfixes ten and twenty men at a shot though they be on the farther side of the mountain. His arrows overwhelm an enemy at more than sixteen thousand feet. It is Juchi Khassar."

Finally, on seeing Genghis Khan's youngest brother in furious action, Bai Bukha turned once more to Jamukha, asking who he was.

"That is Temuge Ochigin, the youngest son of Oelun. Some call him indolent because he likes to take to his couch early and to lie there late, but in the hour of battle he is never backward."

When the Naimans had been forced to retreat to the very top of Mount Naku, Jamukha deserted. He sent a message to Genghis, telling him how he had filled the T'ai-yang with fear. But if he had hoped to gain favor with his sworn brother, he failed. Genghis Khan ignored the message. Jamukha escaped during the night. He led his followers deep into the Altai Mountains, where he joined Kuchluk, who had also escaped and sought haven with his uncle.

Bai Bukha was mortally wounded during the night, and he died before morning. The brave Khorisu Bechi rallied his officers and men and tried to break out of the Mongol army's clutches by fleeing down the mountain at dawn. They were cut down until not a warrior remained alive.

The great battle of Chakirmaut was over, and Genghis Khan's victory was complete. He now ruled from the Khingan Mountains in the east to the Altai Mountains in the west. He was truly the emperor of Mongolia.

NINE

THE BETRAYER BETRAYED

GENGHIS Khan had disposed of his enemies one by one. He would defeat larger armies and conquer greater territories, but his victory over the Naimans was his most important. It made him master of the steppes, the plateaus, and the barren reaches of all Mongolia. He had restored the Mongol Empire and extended its power.

Some Naimans escaped and fled into the Altai Mountains, eventually to rejoin Kuchluk. Many were killed; others surrendered and became subjects of Genghis Khan. The Khatakins, Durbens, Saljiuds, and Keraits all went over to Genghis. The beautiful Princess Gurbesu, favorite wife of Bai Bukha, was among the prisoners captured, and Genghis Khan took her for his own.

Some Mergids, Oirads, and Tatars escaped, as did the princes Altan and Kuchar. But in the vast reaches of Mongolia, stretching from the Altai to the Khingan Mountains, Genghis Khan's enemies had been reduced to such a weak force that Genghis had no longer any fear of attack. He could well afford to rest his valiant and fearless cavalry. They deserved it after their long march and tremendous victory.

Genghis spent the year 1205 in consolidating his gains. Newly conquered clans were merged with his own. Strong organization and communications lines were established. Genghis brought his Mongol Empire under firm control.

Genghis Khan was also elevated to the title of khaghan, which he never used, at a second kurultai held in 1206. He was thirty-nine years old. The *Yüan Ch'ao Pi Shih* records this great gathering with the words, "And so, when all the generations living in felt tents became united under a single authority, in the year of the Leopard [1206], they assembled near the sources of the Onon, and raising the White Banner on Nine Legs, they conferred on Genghis the title Khagan."

Of this same kurultai, Vladimirtsov writes, "Chingis-khan introduced a definite religious idea into the political conception of his own suzerainty and of that of his clan. A prominent part of the kurultai of 1206 was played by the sorcerer Shaman Kukchu, son of Munglik, whom the Mongols viewed with superstitious reverence. Kukchu announced that the Everlasting Blue Sky favored Chingis-khan, who was its own preordained envoy on earth and all his clan. Chingis himself readily accepted the view. 'The Sky has ordered me to govern all peoples,' he said. 'With the protection of the Everlasting Sky I defeated the Keraits and attained to supreme rank.' The White Banner on Nine Legs was now inhabited by the guardian genius (Sulde) of Chingis' own clan (the Borjigin). The Sulde would protect his troops and lead them to victory; he would conquer all peoples for the Everlasting Blue Sky. To this day the Mongols preserve and revere the White Banner of the Sulde, which is the same, they believe, that led the armies of Chingis-khan from victory to victory. They believe that the soul of the great emperor has itself entered this Sulde banner, and that he has himself become the guardian genius of his glorious clan."

The generosity of Genghis Khan and his use of gifts to hold his empire in tight control is suggested in one statement from the Bilik, the maxims of Genghis Khan, fragments of which have come down through seven centuries. "My bowmen and warriors," he stated, "loom like a thick forest; their wives, sweethearts and maidens shine like red flames. My task is to sweeten their mouths with gifts of sweet sugar, to decorate their breasts, backs and shoulders with garments of brocade, to seat them on good geldings, give them to drink from pure and sweet rivers, provide their beasts with good and abundant pastures, and to order that the great roads and highways that serve as ways for the people to be kept clean."

In handing out gifts, Genghis Khan appointed ninety-five of his most valiant officers as "commander of one thousand," especially chosen warriors who went into battle only when Genghis himself was in the thick of the fighting. His grandson Kublai was made senior commander of the army, and Jebe and Subudei were given the ranks of chief with large followings of their own.

The greatest honors went to Bugurji and Mukhali. Bugurji was made commander-in-chief of the west, or right wing. Mukhali was named commander-in-chief of the east, or left wing. Thus, Bugurji controlled the armies from the center of Mongolia to the Altai Mountains, and Mukhali commanded the armies from the center to the Khingan Mountains.

Genghis Khan reserved his greatest awards for his family. Of the thousands and thousands of families he had captured, he gave ten thousand families apiece to his mother and his youngest brother, Temuge Ochigin. His son Juchi was given nine thousand families, Jaghati, eight thousand, Ugedei, five thousand, and Tului, five thousand. His brother Juchi Khassar was given two thousand families, and his half brother Bulgutai one thousand five hundred families.

With these gifts and the distribution of honors to his most trusted officers, Genghis Khan firmly cemented their loyalty to him and his control over them.

Many months passed by as Genghis was putting his house in solid order. Then once more he marched west toward the Altai to rid himself forever of the remaining Mergids and Naimans who still held out against him. These were minor campaigns. With warriors and horses well rested, Genghis had little difficulty in overcoming the opposition.

On his return east, Genghis Khan had his final meeting with his oldest and most persistent enemy, Jamukha, who had been forced to live in hiding with only a few of his Jajirads still with him. He had become a bandit, raiding small and unprotected clans for his daily needs. Learning that the great Genghis Khan was passing near them, Jamukha's bandits, believing that they would be highly rewarded if they took their leader to the Mongol Khan, betrayed Jamukha and delivered him bound in a yoke to Genghis.

The bandits quickly learned how Genghis Khan rewarded disloyalty. The account of this final meeting appears in the *Yüan Ch'ao Pi Shih.*

" 'Is it possible to leave alive men who have betrayed their lord!' " were Genghis Khan's wrathful words. " 'Let them be put to death with their sons and grandsons.' "

Genghis looked now on his sworn brother and long-time enemy. He offered to renew their early relationship when they had first become anda.

Jamukha rejected the offer, and replied:

" 'In those days long ago when we became sworn brothers, we cooked our food and ate together; we spoke words to one another that cannot be forgotten. Then came people between us who set us against one another. Remembering those old words, I grow red with shame and have not the courage to face my sworn brother. You wish me to be your comrade, but though I bear the name, in fact I should not be so. Today, you have gathered people under your rule and there is no way I can be your comrade. If you don't slay me, I shall always be like a louse on your collar or a spine in your inner gate. Because of me you will be uneasy by day, and at night will sleep fitfully. Your mother has wisdom; you are a hero; your brothers have talent; your comrades are valiant knights; you have seventy-three geldings in your great lords. But I from childhood have had neither parents nor brothers; my wife is a babbler; my comrades not trusty; so my sworn brother, above whom is the Sky, has surpassed me. Now grant that I may die quickly that my brother's heart be at peace, and that I may die without the shedding of blood. Then after death, I will forever be the protector and helper of your descendants.' "

To die without bloodshed was considered important by the Mongols, for they believed that a man's soul lived in his blood. There are two versions as to how Jamukha was executed without bloodshed. One states that he was crushed to death. The other says that he was strangled with a silken bowstring.

The princes Altan and Kuchar were reported to have been killed in skirmishes at the same time. Now there was no one in all Mongolia who could openly defy the power and rule of Genghis Khan.

But trouble still pursued the Mongol. This time it came from within his own clan.

TEN

DEATH OF A SORCERER

SHAMANS, sorcerers, and diviners were highly respected in the Mongol religion. They were a superstitious people, and they followed the lead and advice of their shamans almost as they followed their ruler—but not quite.

During the great kurultai of 1206, the shaman Kukchu had played an important role in proclaiming Genghis Khan as the preordained envoy on earth of the "Everlasting Blue Sky." Since that time, Genghis had frequently consulted with Kukchu, who believed his influence over Genghis to be so great that he took an ever-increasing part in the affairs of state. And he wanted even more. He had a bitter quarrel with Juchi Khassar, after which he came to Genghis and, according to Vladimirtsov, said, "The Spirit has revealed to me a holy command of the Everlasting Sky; first Temuchin will rule over the nations, and after him Khassar. If you do not eliminate Khassar your cause is in jeopardy."

As superstitious as any of his people, Genghis Khan

69

called his brother before him and stripped him of his command. Juchi Khassar was greatly humiliated. Genghis planned to go even further and deprive his brother of the two thousand families he had given him, but at this point Oelun Eke—calmer, wiser, less superstitious—stepped in. She reasoned with Genghis, and the Mongol confessed to his mother that he had been afraid. After long conversations with Oelun Eke, Genghis restored his brother's authority. But, perhaps fearful of complete defiance of the message that Kukchu said had come from the Everlasting Blue Sky, Genghis took back six hundred families from his brother.

Still, Kukchu did not give up. He turned his attention to Temuge Ochigin, insulting him with the vilest words that he could use against the Khan's youngest brother.

Burte pleaded with her husband to take action against the shaman. Genghis, although suspicious and fearful of Kukchu, was even more fearful of any threat to the stability of his rule. Therefore, he gave Temuge Ochigin free reign to deal with Kukchu. A few days later, the shaman visited the yurt of Genghis Khan. Temuge stationed three strong wrestlers to wait outside until Kukchu emerged. When he did, the wrestlers seized him and broke his back, tossing his lifeless body aside.

This act, the murder of a shaman, the sorcerer who had direct communication with the Everlasting Blue Sky, caused the more superstitious of the Mongols to voice their disapproval. Their murmurings grew to a clamor, and Genghis Khan was forced to act. According to Vladimirtsov, the Khan, "in order to quiet public opinion excited by the murder of the famous shaman made the following notable statement: 'Tab Tangri beat my brothers and slandered them iniquitously. That is why the Sky withdrew its love from him, and with it his life and body.' In his statement Genghis pointed out clearly that the Sky favored and continued favoring himself and his clan, and was prepared to punish anyone who attempted to rise against the Khan of the Mongols, or his kin."

Genghis then summoned Munglik, Kukchu's father, and said to him: "You failed to teach your own sons. He wished to be equal to me, that is why I undid him. If I had foreseen such qualities in you and yours, I would have undone all of you long ago. But if, after giving one's word in the morning, one were to change it by nightfall, or after giving it in the evening, withdrew it in the morning, one would be brought to shame by the judgement of men; I have promised to free you from death. So let there be an end to the matter."

All his life, as seen in his handling of Kukchu's treachery, Genghis Khan stressed his demand for loyalty. Never would he put up with disloyalty, opposition, or any attempts at interference by anyone—even the most exalted personage.

Order had been restored. There were no enemies left in Mongolia to threaten the great conqueror and ruler. His army was rested; his horses were fat. The Khan had brought all the nomad tribes and clans of the north under his firm control. But still he could not rest. He desired more power, more booty. So he made plans to strike at the south, toward Hsi Hsia and the kingdom of the Chin.

Knowing that he was going against the strongest enemy he had ever faced, Genghis Khan carefully reviewed his army. There must be no weaknesses. His warriors must be at their best. His horses must be rested, strong, and most of all, plentiful. There was plenty of food and weapons. The Mongol Empire was a smoothly operating organization. Genghis had no fear of leaving its administration in the hands of his appointed officials. Everyone knew how he handled those who were disloyal.

The emperor of Mongolia was now ready to expand his rule.

ELEVEN

THE MONGOL ARMY AND THE HUNT

IT WAS the Mongol army, a perfectly tuned machine of war, that made the Mongols a military power unmatched in history until the twentieth century. Not even Attila and his great barbaric hordes conquered as much territory as did the Mongols under their great leader. History has never recorded such skill in open fighting as that of the Mongol warriors swooping down upon an adversary.

The Mongol army is history's outstanding example of the possibilities of nomadic warfare. Its victorious sweep of all its opponents is a testament to the greatness of its leader. By his sheer personality and personal prowess, his wily skill, his triumphs over discouraging setbacks in his youth, Genghis Khan welded numerous nomadic tribes into one great confederacy that was to rule half the world. By the rigorous discipline he exerted over his warriors, he was able to defeat much larger and stronger nations on his relentless march toward the domination of all of Asia and part of Europe.

73

The Mongols did not gain their great and numerous victories by the force of sheer numbers. More often than not, the army won out over foes much greater in numerical strength. Attila the Hun was able to ravage Europe eight centuries earlier by the overwhelming numbers of his barbaric hordes. Genghis Khan won Asia by his skill.

The Mongols' superiority over more civilized armies is attributed to mobility, coordination, outstanding leadership, and what would today be called staff work. Perhaps most important was the excellence of their lines of communication. Large columns of warriors were dispersed over areas hundreds of miles apart. They moved rapidly over the most rugged terrain; yet despite the great distances separating the columns, they maintained a coordination of movement that brought all forces together at exactly the right time and place. This was made possible by the excellence of the Mongols' courier service, their highly developed advance and flank scouting; and the unbelievable hardihood of the Mongol warrior and his horse.

Not until the end of the nineteenth century, six hundred years later, did European armies develop comparable communications or demonstrate feats of coordination as great as those of the Mongols.

The Mongol warrior was of average height. He appeared to be broad and stocky in body, partly due to his heavy sheepskin coat and his thick leather boots. His hardiness was his outstanding feature. Neither the heat

74

of the desert nor the bitter cold of the winter seemed to affect him. His endurance was amazing. Forced marches were measured in degrees of longitude and latitude rather than in miles. Mongol warriors, according to Marco Polo, frequently slept while mounted and armed, as their horses grazed. It was nothing for a warrior to go for ten days without eating cooked food. At these times, he lived on his "iron" ration, consisting of kumiss, dried milk curd, and a small amount of cured meat. If his food supply ran out, he would eat vultures, or seize carrion from the vultures, eating the rotting meat with no ill effect. As a final measure, to quell the ravishes of hunger, the Mongol would open a vein in his horse's neck and suck the blood.

The warrior's principal weapon was the bow and arrow. The bow was quite large and required a pull of one hundred and sixty-six pounds, much more than that required for the famed English longbow. The arrows could kill at distances up to three hundred yards, three times the length of a football field. Marco Polo wrote that two types of arrows were used. Light arrows with small, razor-sharp points were used for long distances and for pursuit. Heavier arrows with large, wide heads were used for close-quarter combat. In battle the warriors carried thirty arrows of each type in their quivers.

Other weapons included a lightweight, short saber and long and short lances. Both kinds of lances had a hook just behind the tip. The hook was used to drag the enemy

75

off his horse. Attached to the warrior's saddle was a mace, a heavy spiked club, used for smashing through armor.

The Mongol warrior wore a steel cap helmet. It had a leather neckpiece of hide or overlapping iron scales wired together. Both men and horses wore this armor. Four kinds of shields were used: a light shield of willow-covered skin for sentry duty; a small shield carried by troops in the foot vanguard to ward off enemy arrows; a shield worn as a visor; and a large heavy shield used when assaulting a walled city.

General field equipment included a file to sharpen arrows, a hatchet, lasso, rope for pulling engines of war, a watertight leather bag for keeping clothes dry when fording rivers, two leather bottles, and a fur or sheepskin cloak and a fur helmet to be worn in extreme cold. A small tent was allotted to each ten warriors.

The Mongol horse was as remarkable as his rider. The animal was considered unequaled throughout the world for its stamina. It stood thirteen to fourteen hands high, and was grass-fed and watered once a day. It is recorded that a Mongol warrior could cover six hundred miles over the most rugged terrain in nine days. When greater speed was needed, as in the courier service, the rider led spare mounts, changing from one to another at the first sign of the horse's tiring.

Genghis Khan placed so much importance on communications that his couriers had road rights which were never questioned. They traveled along a well-kept network of roads that had been developed from caravan routes. Along these paths at regular intervals were stations, called *yams*. A courier riding up to a yam was immediately supplied with a fresh saddled horse. In minutes, the courier was on his way again. Anything he might request was instantly supplied.

Mongol horses were not broken until they were three years old. They were trained to allow an archer to fire his arrows at full gallop. They were also trained to stand as a shield as a dismounted archer fired from behind the horse. When it was possible, a horse ridden one day was rested for the next three days.

The Mongol saddle was made of wood. Daily rubbing with sheep fat prevented it from swelling. The saddle weighed about ten pounds and had a high back and front, permitting a warrior to remain firm in his seat at any speed and fire his arrows in any direction.

All Mongol boys were strapped to the saddle at the age of three. It is no wonder that they were such superb horsemen.

The Mongol army was divided into three main territorial groups. The army of the left wing controlled all territory in the east. The right wing ruled the territory in the west, and the army of the center formed the imperial ordus, or guard. These armies were formed on the decimal basis. The strongest single unit corresponding to the modern-day division was called a *tumen*, and was made up of ten thousand warriors. When two or more tumens were put together, they formed an army. The tumens were subdivided into units of ten regiments of one thousand warriors each. These were broken down into ten squadrons of one hundred warriors each, and these in turn were divided into units (*arbans*) of ten troops each. No warrior was permitted to transfer from one unit to another.

The main units were commanded by kinsmen of Genghis Khan or by close associates in whom he placed full trust. These commanders placed their own kinsmen as heads of the smaller units under them, and this process was repeated down to the smallest unit. Thus, from tumen down to arban there was a continuity of command based on either kinship or loyalty to the next in line.

As the highest in authority, an army commander was given a huge drum. Only he could sound the drum or order it sounded. When Genghis Khan was with an army, it did not move unless he so ordered. These orders were issued under the standard of the nine white yak tails.

The imperial guard was made up of the finest troops in the Mongol army. The guard was first formed in 1203, when Genghis conquered the Keraits. At that time it was composed of seventy warriors as the day guard and eighty men for night duty. In addition there were four hundred archers and a personal guard of one thousand, who became the advance unit when the Khan led his army into battle.

78

The size of the guard was increased when Genghis became the supreme ruler of Mongolia at the council of 1206. Announcing that since the Everlasting Blue Sky had ordered him to rule all nations, he brought the guard's strength up to ten thousand. Genghis insisted that the men of the guard be members of the nobility. He demanded that they be "well-built, agile, and hardy." All male Mongols from the ages of fourteen to sixty were subject to military service. In times of peace, which were rare, all males had to participate in the annual hunt.

The annual hunt served two purposes. The first was to provide food for the long winter months when game was scarce, and second, the hunt was carried out as a military campaign with all the care and detail that went into a battle. The major military tactic of the Mongols was encirclement of the enemy, and this encirclement tactic was well learned during the annual hunt.

The hunt usually took place in the fall of the year if the Mongol army was not waging war. For a month— often two months—the Mongols formed a great circle covering hundreds of square miles on the steppes and mountains. The circle surrounded an area as large as the state of Connecticut.

The rim of the circle was marked by the bright-colored standards of the Mongol regiments. In the center, called the *gurtai*, a standard was planted. When the game— thousands of deer, bear, tigers, wolves, leopards, and

79

smaller animals—were herded in around the gurtai, then —and not until then—the kill could begin.

Mongol warriors were posted only feet apart around the entire great circle. Couriers dashed madly along the rim, urging a regiment forward or holding another back. The circle had to close as slowly and as perfectly as possible. Signal fires were built.

As the cordon slowly closed, day by day, contracting on the frightened animals, the danger to the warriors increased. They were not permitted to use their weapons. Anyone who disobeyed this order was put to death. A charging tiger had to be turned back by shouts, by hurled stones, by bare hands if necessary. To permit an animal to escape through the cordon was a disgrace.

Throughout the entire hunt, couriers brought daily reports to Genghis Khan, telling him how it was going.

Beaters thrashed through underbrush and swamp, driving the animals ever inward toward the center. No excuse was allowed for the nature of the terrain. Ravines, gullies, marshes, rivers, and lakes were not considered excusable obstacles. Warriors pursued the beasts through these dangerous areas, and many men and many animals perished.

As the circle contracted, its ring of men grew thicker and thicker, two deep, three deep. Finally as the circle closed, the snarling animals were crowded body to body. The thousands of warriors forming the hunt were a mass of men, hundreds deep.

At this point in the hunt, Genghis Khan rode forward. A lane opened for him leading to what was now an arena filled with vicious, frightened animals. Genghis always made the first kill. Skilled with bow and arrow, he would select a leaping deer and send a deadly arrow through its heart. The fall of the deer was the signal for the princes and noblemen to make their kills. When they retired from the arena, Genghis gave the signal for his horde of warriors to finish off the game. The horde surged forward, thousands upon thousands of game-hungry warriors, excited by the hunt. The slaughter of the remaining animals might go on for days, until there remained only a few of each type of beast. These were permitted to escape so that they might breed more game for the next great hunt.

When the hunt ended, the game was cured and stored away against the lean winter months stretching ahead.

After the hunters returned to their home grazing lands, Genghis Khan called the leaders of the hunt before him. These were the princes, noblemen, and officers who led the Mongol army and hunted the enemy. The Khan gave his remarks and criticism of how the hunt had been handled with all the seriousness that was given to the tactics employed in a major battle.

Genghis planned each military campaign with extreme care. The slightest detail was given minute consideration. When it was decided to launch a campaign, a kurultai was called. All top-ranking officers gathered around their leader. Men were selected to go as spies into the enemy's territory. They were to learn not only the military strength of the foe but the political and economic condition of the nation to be attacked. Of greatest importance was accurate information about fortified towns, roads, passes, rivers, and fords. It was indeed a rare occasion when Genghis Khan struck at an enemy without knowing as much about him as the enemy knew about himself.

When the necessary information was brought back to the Mongol leader, the plan of campaign was carefully drawn up. How many men would be needed? How many horses? Usually there were three horses for each warrior. Supplies were of utmost importance. How large a herd of cattle should be driven behind the advancing army so that the warriors might have red meat? What season of the year was best for the strike?

If the campaign was to be waged in an area far removed from the Mongols' main camp, the spies and scouts were required to determine food supplies in the area. To drive herds of cattle great distances would slow up the army's advance and advertise its coming to the enemy. This exacting attention to detail was one reason for Genghis Khan's great success.

One other ruse was always employed by the Mongol leader. Weeks, sometimes only days, before an actual attack was launched, Mongol spies entered the enemy's camp and spread rumors of the great strength of the attacking army. These rumors always highly exaggerated the numerical strength of the invaders. In one campaign, Genghis Khan's forces numbered only forty thousand warriors, yet his spies were so successful that the enemy believed he was leading a horde of one hundred thousand against them.

The encirclement tactic developed in the annual hunt was almost always employed when the Mongols entered an enemy country. Large columns of warriors, separated by fifty to seventy-five miles, approached the enemy country on the right and left. In the center, a smaller vanguard made first contact with the enemy, evaluated its strength, and sent word back by courier.

Genghis Khan, immediately in the rear of this advance force, would study the reports and decide when the time would be right for a full strike. The decision made, couriers dashed to right and left, ordering the columns to move in for the battle. The widely separated divisions of the army closed in with unbelievable speed. Their fast, well-trained horses gave them a mobility that threw into confusion the slower moving, concentrated army of the enemy. The timed thrusts of the Mongol columns brought a succession of victories unmatched in history.

Basically, the Mongol army's victories were due to the seemingly inherent military genius of those remarkable warriors and to the outstanding leadership of their generals. However, as the Mongols chalked up victory after victory, they readily adapted any weapon or method of attack which was an improvement on their own. The catapult and the cataphract (a heavily armored catapult) are two examples of this. The use of flaming naphtha hurled into a walled city is another.

The art of the siege was unknown to the Mongols when Genghis Khan was forming his empire. His warriors quickly learned it when they invaded China. They also used prisoners of war, forcing their captives to lead parties storming the walls of a besieged city. In the capture of Nishapur in Khurasan, the heart of Muslim power in the East, the Mongols made effective use of prisoners taken in preceding battles. The prisoners were forced to build siege engines at the walls of the city under heavy fire from the city's defenders. Then these same captives were driven ahead of the Mongols assaulting the city's walls. Nishapur fell to the Mongols in less than a month.

In this siege, the Mongols used three thousand prisoner-built ballistae (machines for hurling heavy javelins), three thousand catapults, and seven hundred war engines for hurling naphtha. In addition, the captives built four thousand ladders, and brought three thousand loads of boulders from the nearby mountains. The Mongols, driving the captives ahead of them, carried on their assaults relentlessly. The moat surrounding Nishapur was soon filled with the dead bodies of the prisoners. The main force of the Mongols, riding over the bridge of dead bodies, breached the city's walls in seventy places. Once inside the city, every defender met death by a Mongol sword.

In the open field, when the Mongol army met an enemy far superior in number, as was often the case, they employed a ruse. Stuffed dummies were lashed into the saddles of spare horses, doubling or tripling, in the eyes of the enemy, the size of the invading Mongol army.

In every battle of every carefully planned campaign, the Mongol army grew in military knowledge and fighting strength. Genghis Khan and his hordes gained their first knowledge of how war was waged in the more civilized nations when the army marched south, seeking the first of its many victories in China.

TWELVE

MONGOLS INVADE CHINA

Now the absolute ruler of all Mongolia, Genghis Khan turned his triumphant armies toward China. His main objective was the Chin empire, but first he would test his warriors against the weaker kingdom of Hsi Hsia.

China, in the first decade of the thirteenth century, was not a unified nation, but was made up of several small empires and kingdoms. Of these the most powerful was the Chin, and its emperor was recognized as the greatest on earth.

It was Genghis Khan's purpose to show the world that he, not Madaku, emperor of the Chin, was the greatest reigning monarch. He wanted to force the Chin to pay tribute to him, and show to the world that he was the overlord of Madaku.

The Mongol also realized that his restless warriors could be more readily kept in fighting trim if they knew that great stores of booty would be theirs if they successfully invaded the richer and more civilized countries in China.

Madaku, growing alarmed at the strength of the Mongol nation on his northern border, sent an embassy to Genghis Khan, supposedly to collect tribute but actually to get more information about the strength of the Mongols. The embassy got no tribute from Genghis. In fact, the embassy was coldly received and treated with minimum courtesy. The Chin ambassador, Madaku's uncle, Yun-chi, prince of Wei, arrived at Genghis Khan's court even as the Mongol ruler was preparing his army for an invasion.

Alarmed, Yun-chi hurried back to Madaku and advised him to strike at once. But the advice was never followed. Madaku died suddenly; affairs in the Chin Empire were in great disorder and would remain that way until a new emperor could be named.

Genghis Khan did not take advantage of this disordered state. Never before had his warriors faced armies of such great strength as they would face in China, and the Mongol wanted to feel his way by striking first at Hsi Hsia, just north of the Chin Empire.

Twice before, in 1205 and 1207, Genghis Khan had sent small expeditions into Hsi Hsia. These were probes to feel out the enemy and to build up his warriors' hunger for loot.

The Hsi Hsia kingdom was ruled by Li An-ch'uan, emperor of the Tanguts. His army of some one hundred and sixty thousand troops was made up of cavalry and infantry. The invading Mongols were far inferior in strength, probably numbering less than one hundred thousand. The Mongols also had to march over six hundred and fifty miles before reaching enemy territory. This long march was across four hundred and fifty miles of the sands of the Gobi Desert, where grazing was scarce. Weeks before the Mongol army began its long march, herds of sheep were placed at regular intervals to feed the hungry warriors as they marched on the enemy.

Li An-ch'uan sent out a force of fifty thousand men under the command of his nephew Li Tsun-hsiang and General Kao Liang-hui to meet the invader and check his advance. The Tanguts marched north and met the Mongols at the town of Wu-la-hai, near the northern border, in the spring of 1209. They clashed in a fierce but short battle. The Mongols overwhelmed the Tanguts, and captured Prince Li Tsun-hsiang. When General Kao Liang-hui refused to bow to the great Genghis Khan, his head was cut off.

The first battle was won with such ease that Genghis pressed on quickly, penetrating deep into the heart of Hsi Hsia. Li An-ch'uan now massed an army of one hundred and twenty thousand across the plains between the Mongols and his capital, Chung-hsing. The troops held the Mongols back for a time, but they failed to take the offensive and dug into their defense positions.

Two months of sporadic fighting followed, but the

Tanguts, under General Wei-ming Ling-Kung, refused to launch a full-scale offensive. Genghis Khan was satisfied with this failure to act. The Mongols were always at their best fighting on open plains, and their great mobility enabled them to crush much larger forces. When Wei-ming Ling-Kung refused to come out and fight, Genghis resorted to trickery. In full view of the enemy, he struck camp and marched away, leaving but a small detachment as his rear guard. He did not march very far—just out of sight of the enemy—and his warriors lay in ambush behind protective scrub trees and heavy shrubbery.

Wei-ming Ling-Kung was completely taken in, and he moved out to crush the small rear guard. He chased them straight into Genghis Khan's ambush. The Mongols leaped from their concealment, mounted their fast, strong horses, and swept through the Tanguts. The battle was vicious, but by day's end the Tanguts were forced to flee and Wei-ming Ling-Kung was taken prisoner.

Genghis quickly pursued the enemy, and the following day drew up before Chung-hsing (the present town of Ninghsia, or Yinchuan, in China). This was a walled city on the great Yellow River, fed by a series of irrigation canals. These canals, plus the protecting wall surrounding the city, made its capture extremely difficult.

Another two months passed without the Mongols gaining any ground. They were not accustomed to fighting an enemy within a walled city, and no tricks or ruses would bring the Tanguts out into the open.

Genghis Khan reviewed the situation with his generals, and came up with a plan that brought near catastrophe to the city. The Yellow River was swollen by the autumn rains, its waters spilling over its banks. Genghis ordered a huge dike built. The dike turned the waters of the river into the city itself. The flood swept through, destroying life and property and crumbling the protective walls.

The Mongols sat back and let the angry river waters do what they had been unable to do. The strategy worked, but then nearly backfired. The dike burst and the Mongol army had to flee to higher ground, losing many horses and warriors.

When the waters had subsided, Genghis Khan sent a Tangut prisoner to Li An-ch'uan to make certain demands, which, if not met, would result in the Mongols' taking over the city. The Tangut ruler feared that his weakened city would be ravaged by the fierce Mongols. He met the terms and sent a reply to Genghis Khan, which, according to the *Yüan Cha'ao Pi Shih*, amounted to complete capitulation. "Having heard of your glory," the Tangut emperor's message stated, "we were greatly afraid, but now we will be your right hand and will serve you faithfully and will supply you with the products of our realm—camels, woolen cloth, and falcons." As a further peace offering, he gave Genghis Khan one of his daughters.

The Khan had successfully completed his first campaign outside his own Mongolian Empire, and had done so with an army much inferior to that of the enemy. He now felt that he could move against the far stronger Chin Empire.

Genghis was forty-three years old in 1210, when he completed his successful invasion of Hsi Hsia. Deep lines etched the tough, sunburned skin of his broad face. On his head he wore tall eagle feathers attached to a red band, with red streamers dangling from it down his back. He wore a long-sleeved black sable coat, bound at the middle with a broad band of gold discs. He sat in his high saddle in short stirrups, his knees hunched up. Slowly he rode up and down the long lines of his warriors standing in review. He spoke little, a word of praise for this general, a sharp word of criticism for another.

Genghis Khan withdrew from Hsi Hsia westward to rest his warriors and plan his campaign against the Chin. While in camp he was visited by a Chin embassy. It was the embassy's mission to inform the Mongol that a new "son of heaven" had ascended the Chin throne, succeeding the late Madaku. The chief envoy said that the Khan must now make a *kowtow* to the new son of heaven. And who was the new son of heaven? Genghis asked. It was Yun-chi, the prince of Wei, now Wei Shao Wang, son of heaven, emperor of the Chin. Instead of kowtowing— kneeling and touching his forehead to the ground— Genghis Khan turned to the south, facing the Chin

Empire, and spat. There would be no kowtowing on the part of the Mongolian emperor.

Plans for the second invasion of China were completed in February, 1211. They called for a simultaneous strike at the Chin Empire at two widely separated points. The center and left wings of the Mongol army would break into the empire near the Huan Chou area; the army of the right wing would strike further south, near Ching Chou. (Both locations are in the present Chinese province of Suiyuan, directly south of Mongolia.)

The left wing and central armies were commanded by Genghis, Mukhali (the general-in-chief of the left wing), and Jebe, Subudei, Juchi Khassar, and Tului. The right wing was commanded by princes Juchi, Jaghatai, and Ugedei, and by Genghis' great friend, Bugurji.

A third force of some twenty-five thousand warriors, under Temuge Ochigin, was left to guard Mongolia.

The left wing and central armies numbered some seventy thousand warriors; the right wing had forty thousand. The invading Mongol army was going against a Chin force of five hundred thousand.

The Mongols quickly crossed the Gobi and entered the friendly territory of the Onguds. Alakush Tagin, chieftain of the Onguds, had once before offered his help to Genghis, when the Mongols defeated the Naimans. Now he offered Genghis additional troops and threw open his grazing lands for the thousands of sheep that the Mongol army brought with it. In return for this demonstrated friendship, Genghis Khan gave his daughter, Alaghi Beki, to Alakush Tagin's eldest son. If the Khan's numerical strength was weak his positional strength was strong. The Onguds bordered the Chin Empire. Genghis was able to rest his warriors in friendly territory, ready to break into the Chin lands when he felt the right moment had come.

While Genghis Khan rested the main body of his troops, smaller columns under Jebe and Subudei easily penetrated Huan Chou and captured it. Ching Chou was as easily taken by detachments under Juchi, Jaghatai, and Ugedei.

The Chin massed its main army, directly opposing Genghis Khan. Before the battle, over two hundred miles separated the left wing and central armies, and the right wing. When the battle began, the right wing closed the wide gap with amazing swiftness, and despite the overwhelming numerical superiority of the Chin, Genghis carried the day. The enemy could not match the superior leadership of the Mongols, and military historians say the Chin badly mishandled their troops.

Genghis Khan was victorious in this first meeting, but the Chin were by no means done. The second and longer phase of the war between the Mongols and the Chin would soon begin. First, however, Genghis Khan marched north, to rest his warriors and replenish his cavalry with fresh horses.

THIRTEEN

THE CONQUEST OF CHINA

IN the autumn of 1212, Genghis Khan moved back to the attack. Two forces marched across the border of the Chin Empire, one under the command of Genghis, the second under Prince Tului.

In one battle, the Mongol lured the Chin, commanded by Ao Tun-hsiang, into a valley, encircled the army, and nearly wiped it out. The Chin general barely made his escape, and retreated with the remnants of his once-strong army.

The conqueror now laid siege to the walled city of Hsi Ching. Mongol casualties were high because the invaders were just beginning to learn the art of the siege. During this attack, Genghis was seriously wounded by an arrow fired by a bowman from the city walls. Genghis raised the siege and moved his army back north.

Prince Tului and his army in the east were turned back on their first assault on Te-hsing, but returned to the attack and breached the walls. The loot-hungry Mongols poured through and sacked the city. Tului did not carry on his attack. He withdrew and joined his father in the north.

In July of the following year, 1213, the Khan launched his third invasion of the Chin Empire. This one was marked by almost continuous fighting for two years, with only brief respites when Genghis rested his battle-weary warriors, renewed his supplies, and had mounts sent down from Mongolia for his cavalry.

To the east, across the provinces of Hopei, Shenshi, and Shansi, lay Chung Tu (modern-day Peking), the Chin capital. Toward this goal Genghis Khan marched his armies.

Te-hsing, abandoned by Prince Tului, had been reoccupied by the Chin. The Mongols quickly reduced the city for a second time. Next the Mongol emperor scored a smashing victory in the valley of Wei-ch'uan (present-day Huai-lai) by employing the encircling tactic of the hunt.

Genghis Khan threw his central army at the massed forces of the Chin, commanded by Chu-hu Kao-chi and Wan-yeng Kang, holding it in check. Two wings of the Mongol army, one under Prince Tului, the other under Chugu, an adopted son of the conqueror, skirted either side of the enemy army, striking the Chin's flanks and rear.

Tightening their circle as they did in the hunt, the Mongols slashed at the Chin army until the battle field was strewn with the dead. The Chin fled in panic, retreating to the fortress of Chu-yung Kuan, where they dug in. When after a month of unsuccessful siege the Chu-yung Kuan garrison refused to surrender, Genghis Khan abandoned the siege and moved farther to the east, on the road to the Chin capital.

Victory followed victory on Genghis Khan's relentless march eastward. As the imperial cities of the Chin Empire fell, treachery and a palace revolution among the Chin aided the Mongol's oncoming.

The Chin emperor appointed Chih-chung as vice-commander of the empire. He was given five thousand especially chosen troops as a guard to protect the capital city from within its walls. Chih-chung, a restless man, fretted at being confined within the city, and went on a hunting expedition, taking most of his handpicked guard with him.

The emperor was infuriated at being disobeyed, and sent an aide to reprimand Chih-chung. The vice-commander in turn was angered. He killed the aide, and plotted to take over Chung Tu as his own. Coming back to the capital, Chih-chung met the outside guard several miles from the city. He had the guard's commander slain and took over himself.

A further act of treachery got him back into the city. He sent messengers on ahead with the frightening news that the Mongols were nearing the walled city, and he asked to be allowed to enter. The captain of the guard on one of the city's gates was completely taken in and allowed Chih-chung and his followers inside. Chih-chung cut down the palace guard, killing five hundred officers, and captured Wei Shao Wang. A few days later he murdered the emperor.

Although Chih-chung was capable of any treachery to gain his ends, he stopped short of proclaiming himself emperor, knowing that a Chin ruler could only come from royal blood. In October, 1213, Hsüan Tsung became the new emperor, but he was little more than a vassal to Chih-chung.

One month later, Chih-chung was himself a murder victim. His murder resulted from an order he issued that flared back at him.

Genghis Khan had sent a small detachment to probe the defenses of the Chin capital. Chih-chung ordered one of his generals, Kao-ch'i, to attack the Mongol detachment and defeat it under penalty of death. The Mongols were victorious, and Kao-ch'i, knowing that Chih-chung would carry out his threat, sneaked back into the city and personally attacked Chih-chung. He overpowered the vice-commander and decapitated him with his sword. Kao-ch'i carried the severed head to Emperor Hsüan Tsung, and was rewarded by himself being made vice-commander of the empire.

Genghis Khan was drawing near his goal—the Chin capital. He had divided his army into three striking forces. One army, commanded by the princes Juchi,

Jaghatai, and Ugedei, was under orders to capture all the territory of the western part of Hopei Province and Shansi. Juchi Khassar, Jurchedie, and Anchar Noyan were to overrun the country between Chung Tu and the sea. The third army, with Genghis in command, Mukhali and Tului at his side, would ravage the rest of Hopei and Shansi.

With these three areas under complete control, the Mongol conqueror would be able to devote his full attention to the capture of the great walled capital.

Of all the great cities in China, Chung Tu was the largest and best defended. Eighteen miles of forty-foot-high walls surrounded the city. At the top, the walls measured forty feet across, and at the bottom, fifty feet. Three deep moats circled the walls, and nine hundred towers rose above them. From these towers the Chin defenders could hurl huge stones at an invader. Flaming oil would be rained down on those who crossed the three moats and reached the base of the wall. Expert bowmen were stationed in each tower.

Before this strongly fortified city could be reached, the invader must first overcome four forts, located at strategic points outside the walled city. These forts were small cities in themselves. They were walled, covered a square mile, had their own towers, moats, and arsenals, and were well-stocked with supplies.

Catapults were unknown to the Mongols when Genghis Khan united the Mongolian Empire. But they were quickly added to the Mongols' weapons in their China invasion. Heavily armored cataphracts were also added. These could be used close to the walls of a city, and they gave the Mongols increased fire power. The cataphract could hurl heavy missiles. Mongol bowmen stood behind the cataphracts, protected by them, and sped their deadly arrows at the enemy on top of the walls.

The Mongol army, massed all around Chung Tu, overcame the four outside forts with comparative ease. Then they attempted to take the city by storm. Catapults and cataphracts hurled stones and flaming arrows. Huge battering rams smashed against the thick walls. The defenders repulsed the attack, and the Mongols retired.

A second, more devastating attack was launched against Chung Tu. Again the defenders stood off the attack, but damage within the city was tremendous.

Genghis Khan refused to make a third attempt, despite the strong urging of his generals. He had learned from a captured officer who had fallen from the top of the wall that there was much talk of peace within the beleaguered city. The long sieges by the Mongols had caused food supplies to dwindle. Flaming arrows had set parts of the city on fire. In early April, after two months of continuous siege and two attempts to storm the walls, Genghis Khan sent the Tangut A-la-ch'ien into the city with peace proposals. The messages and peace terms are recorded in two Chinese historical works, the *Meng-wu-erh Shi* and the *Yüan Shih*. Genghis Khan's first message to the Chin emperor Hsüng Tsung was: "The whole of Shantung and Hopei are now in my possession while you retain only Chung Tu; God has made you so weak, that should I further molest you, I know not what Heaven would say; I am willing to withdraw my army, but what provisions will you make to still the demands of my officers?"

The Chin emperor met with his ministers to discuss the peace offering. Kao-ch'i, the vice-commander, wanted to launch an all-out attack against the Mongols. "I have heard that both the men and horses of the Mongols are greatly fatigued and suffering from sickness; should we not take this opportunity to fight a decisive battle?"

Wan-yen Fu-hsing, commander of the troops within Chung Tu, was not in favor of an attack. "Our troops," he said "have been collected from every direction and at the last moment. Though they are in the capital, their families are scattered far and wide in the various *lu* [districts] from which they have come. Hence, their loyalty is uncertain. If defeated, they will fly like birds; if victorious, they will at once want to return to their homes and who then will guard the capital? Rather ought we to consider the situation. In my opinion, the best policy is to send an envoy to seek peace. Then, after the enemy has withdrawn, we can take measures for the future."

The Chin emperor favored the course outlined by Fu-hsing. Peace talks ended early in May, and Hsüng Tsung agreed to Genghis' terms. The *Yüan Shih* records that the initial gifts made to Genghis Khan included the daughter of Wei Shao Wang, former emperor, along with five hundred boys and girls as her entourage, three thousand horses, ten thousand liang of gold (about seven hundred pounds), and ten thousand bolts of silk.

By forcing Hsüng Tsung to give him a princess, Genghis Khan inflicted upon the Chin emperor a great humiliation, making him lose face, and, in fact, forcing Hsüng Tsung to acknowledge Genghis Khan as his overlord. This was the great objective which Genghis had sought. The other gifts were token in nature.

All hostilities ended and peace terms were signed. As hostage, the Chin general Wan-yen Fu-hsing went with the Khan on his march to the north. At the Chu-yung pass in the southern extension of the Greater Khingan Mountains, just outside the Great Wall of China, the Chin general was freed. Historians dispute the fate of the thousands of captives whom Genghis Khan took with him. Some say that he cold-bloodedly massacred the prisoners. Others state that they were released with their general.

Within a few days of Genghis Khan's departure for the north, Hsüng Tsung, still fearing the Mongol conqueror, who was still only a relatively short march away from Chung Tu, decided to move his court to the south and establish a capital at K'ai-feng. By this act, Hsüng Tsung acknowledged the end of the Chin as the great power bordering on the Mongol nation. It meant the loss of Inner Mongolia and eventually of Manchuria, also under Chin sovereignty. Chung Tu was left under the rule of Shou Chung, the imperial prince, and General Wan-yen Fu-hsing, who had returned after being released by Genghis Khan.

The Mongol conqueror was back in his camp in Mongolia when, in July, 1214, he learned that the Chin emperor had abandoned the capital city and moved far south to K'ai-feng. This new move infuriated Genghis Khan. He felt that the peace agreement had been broken and that Hsüng Tsung had used the peace only to mislead the Mongol conqueror. Genghis also knew that if what remained of Hsüng Tsung's Chin empire were to be left unmolested, then Hsüng Tsung could rebuild his strength for his eventual return to Chung Tu.

Once more the Mongol army marched south. They made further ravages in Hopei and Shantung provinces on both sides of the Yellow River and, in May of 1215, the entire Mongol army was massed for the second time around the walls of Chung Tu. This time the Mongol conqueror was not to be denied. As the siege continued day after day after day, the Chins inside the walled city came to a point of starvation. It was reported that cannibalism had become common. Chung Tu fell at last to the Mongols. The city was put in command of Shi-mo Ming-an, a former Khitan general, who had been captured by Genghis Khan. He had sworn allegiance and had become one of the Khan's most trusted generals. Genghis again returned to the north.

Ming-an was unable to control the loot-hungry Mongols who twice before had been denied the rich spoils inside the city. Many thousands were slain as the Mongol warriors sacked the capital. For months after, the bones of the dead formed huge hills within the city. The victorious warriors continued their ravages of other sections of the Chin Empire. Although they were unable to capture K'ai-feng and take the Chin emperor as prisoner, the power of the Chin was gone forever.

Had Genghis Khan been able to continue to concentrate his war on the Chin, as he undoubtedly planned to do once his warriors were rested, K'ai-feng and the Chin emperor probably would have become his victims. But his attention was suddenly diverted to the west. War broke out between the Mongols and the Muslim Empire in what is now that part of Soviet Russia southwest of the Aral Sea.

All of China, with the exception of Manchuria, was now under the domain of the Mongols. To bring this vast territory under his sway, Genghis Khan dispatched two armies to cross over the Khinghan Mountains into Manchuria. One army was led by Juchi Khassar; the other by General Mukhali.

Manchuria was conquered in 1220, and, a few years later, Korea was added. Genghis Khan took no personal part in these conquests. He was much too occupied with wars in the west.

FOURTEEN

DESTRUCTION AND DEATH

BEFORE departing for his campaigns in the west, which were to take several years, Genghis Khan bestowed upon General Mukhali the highest honors in his power. He granted him authority far greater than he had given his sons or brothers.

General Mukhali was put in command of all the armies in China. To establish Mukhali's authority as supreme, Genghis Khan, in a formal ceremony, gave his general a white nine-tailed standard and a golden tiger seal of authority, and announced that General Mukhali's orders were to be implicitly obeyed, as if they came from Genghis Khan himself. General Mukhali left his emperor in September, 1217, for his new command. The two were never to meet again.

Mukhali, the greatest of the Mongol conqueror's generals, died a natural death in 1223, while still in China. His dying words, as recorded in the *Meng-wu-erh Shi*, expressed his regret at having failed his emperor in one great task. Speaking to his brother Taisun, he said, "For nearly forty years I have waged war for the Khan, and east and west I have vanquished his enemies that he might bring to completion his great work. But K'ai-feng still remains untaken. This I greatly regret, so see to it that you do your best to take it." Mukhali was fifty-four at his death.

Genghis Khan was still fighting in the west when his great general died. He had been at war almost constantly since he had sent Mukhali east and he himself had led his armies to the west.

Before his invasion of the Muslim Empire of Khorezimian near the Aral Sea, the Khan was forced to deal with one of his oldest enemies. Twelve years before, he had defeated the Naimans on the slopes of the Altai Mountains.

T'ai-yang, chieftain of the Naimans, was killed in the battle, but his son Kuchluk had escaped. In the intervening years, while Genghis Khan was waging war in China, Kuchluk had made alliances with other clans and had built up considerable strength. He made continued forays into the Mongol Empire in the northwest, and was assuming the proportion of a challenger to Genghis Khan's rule of Mongolia.

Kuchluk's aspirations were short-lived, however. The Mongol army overtook his much smaller force and defeated it. The Naiman prince again escaped and fled into the Pamir Mountains, north of the Aral Sea. After several weeks, he was hunted down and beheaded. Genghis Khan ordered that the head of the Naiman prince be carried and displayed through those areas which Kuchluk had so recently ruled. There was no longer any question as to the absolute rule and authority of the Mongol emperor.

With Kuchluk disposed of and his followers once more under the strong army of the Mongol emperor, Genghis Khan was able to direct his full attention to his invasion of the Khorezimian Empire. Plans for this invasion were made as carefully as they had been made for the invasion and conquest of China. Reports had come to Genghis Khan that the Khorezimian leader Khwarazm Shah had a powerful force at his command. Genghis was not able to use his whole army for the invasion, since a large force had to be left behind to control the Mongolian Empire, and a still larger force was with General Mukhali in China. To increase the size of the army he would take south, Genghis Khan called upon his vassals to supply additional troops. All complied but one, the defeated Tanguts of Hsi Hsia.

Li An-ch'uan, leader of the Tanguts, had sworn loyalty to Genghis Khan, promising to be his right hand. But when the Khan's ambassador arrived in the Tangut capital of Chung-hsing, the situation had changed. Li Tsun-hsiang was now the Tangut king, having succeeded on his father's death. The Mongol ambassador made known to the king the desires of Genghis Khan: "You have promised to be my right hand. Now the Muslims have murdered my ambassador and I go to demand satisfaction. You shall be my right hand."

Before the Tangut king could reply, according to the *Yüan Ch'ao Pi Shih*, the foremost Tangut noble, Asha Gano, spoke up, "If your forces are insufficient you need not be khaghan." King Li Tsun-hsiang apparently thought the same, because he refused to send any of his warriors to help Genghis Khan in his invasion of the Khorezimian Empire.

When the ambassador returned to the Mongol camp, Genghis Khan was infuriated by the Tangut's refusal. "How dared Asha Gano speak such words. It would be easy for me to send my army against them at once instead of Khwarazm but I will not now alter my plans, but if heaven helps and preserves me, I will march against them on my return."

Li Tsun-hsiang was to regret his decision, and Genghis Khan was to keep his promise.

Genghis marched on the Khorezimian Empire in 1219. Four years were to pass before he began his long march homeward. In this campaign, in which a great part of the Muslim Empire came under his sovereignty, he completely destroyed the forces of the Khwarazm Shah. His men captured and occuiped Transoxiana, Khwarazm, and the greater part of Khurasan. He left behind him sufficient forces to gain and hold complete control over this newly conquered territory. Two of his generals, Jebe and Subudei, at the close of the Khorezimian campaign, marched farther west, campaigning successfully in Persia, the Caucasus, southeastern Russia, and Bulgaria.

Genghis Khan made a leisurely return east, not reaching the familiar grazing grounds along the Kerulen River until 1225. He remained in camp for the summer of 1226, and made plans for the destruction of Hsi Hsia. He had not forgotten the Tangut king's refusal to send him troops.

In the fall of 1226, Genghis Khan began his second march toward the Hsi Hsia kingdom. The Mongol emperor was now nearly sixty years old, but he rode at the head of his invading troops. He interrupted his march in November to stage a great hunt, which lasted for a month. During the hunt, the emperor's horse was frightened by a wild boar, and Genghis was thrown to the ground. His injuries were quite severe, more so than any of those he had ever received in battle. His generals wanted to return to Mongolia until their leader had fully recovered, but Genghis was against this advice. He felt that if he withdrew now, the Tanguts would interpret his retirement as being afraid to attack. Another month was spent resting until the emperor was able to mount his horse again.

In several skirmishes with the Tanguts during the first months of 1227, the Mongols were completely victorious. The decisive victory came near the city of Ling Chou where the Tanguts had massed one hundred thousand men. Genghis Khan won an overwhelming victory, and the power of the Tanguts was destroyed forever. There remained only mopping-up tactics and the destruction of smaller cities and towns.

Genghis now ordered his warriors to wipe out the entire Tangut race, but before this death sentence could be executed, a soothsayer noticed five constellations coming together in the southwest. He told the Mongol emperor that the omen was very bad, and the Khan rescinded his order. His warriors were to slay only those Tanguts in the front lines, taking the others as prisoners, and leaving women and children alone. There was to be no looting.

Not long after this victory, with the kingdom of Hsi Hsia destroyed as he had promised, Genghis Khan fell seriously ill. Just what his illness was is not known, but it is believed that the heavy fall he had suffered months before may have been the major cause.

After an illness of seven days, the great Mongol leader, who had conquered half the world, died, on August 19, 1227.

The exact place of his death is disputed, there being no fewer than four places named by historians. The most reliable appears to be that in the *Yüan Shih*, the history published in 1317. The *Yüan Shih* states that Genghis Khan died in Hsi Hsia at a campsite on the Hsi River. (The river today is called Ch'ing-shui.)

Even as the Mongol conqueror lay dying, his thoughts

turned to the eventual total conquest of the Chin and the capture of the new capital, K'ai-feng. The *Yüan Shih* gives him the following deathbed words:

> The best troops of the Chin are at T'ung Kuan; to the south they rest on the Lien mountains, on the north they reach the Great [Yellow] River. It is not easy to force this position, but if permission can be obtained to march through the dominions of the Sung, our men can be led via Teng and T'ang and go straight to K'ai-feng. This will place the Chin in a difficult position and compel the withdrawal of many thousand troops from T'ung Kuan. But these, both men and horses, will be exhausted after marching over one thousand li [some three hundred and thirty miles] to the capital, and even if they arrive will be worthless and an easy prey to our men.

A completely different version of Genghis Khan's last words is given by the Persian historian 'Ala-Ad-Din 'Ata-Milki Juvaini. According to Juvaini, Genghis Khan had his sons, Tului and Ugedei, brought before him and said to them:

> I have almost come to my end. For you I have created this empire. To the north, south, east, and west my dominions extend for a year's journey. If you want to retain your possessions and conquer your

110

enemies, you must make your subjects submit willingly and unite your energies to one end, as in that way you may continue to hold your power. When I am gone you must recognize Ugedei as my successor. Further, let each see to his own affairs. During many years I have enjoyed a great name and I die without regrets, but my spirit wishes to return to my native land. Although Jaghatai is not present to hear my words, I do not think he will disobey my wishes and cause a disturbance. I die in the territory of the enemy and though the ruler of Hsi Hsia has submitted, he has not yet arrived. Hence, after I am dead, conceal my death and kill him when he comes.

Li Hsien, who had succeeded his brother as the Tangut king, was brought to the Mongol camp in September, nearly a month after Genghis Khan had died. He brought with him many presents—golden buddhas, horses, camels, gold, silver, and young boys and girls. He was told that Genghis Khan lay ill, and was ordered to bow down before the tent. Then he, his family, and his entourage were slain.

A great cortege was formed to carry the body of the Mongol conqueror to his homeland. The funeral procession was led by General Subudei. The *Altan Tobci* and the *Sanang Setsen,* two Mongol histories written three centuries after the death of Genghis Khan, record that the cortege was led by a Sunid named Kilugen Baa-

tur. As the procession moved north toward the Kerulen
River, Kilugen sang to the spirit of the conqueror:

> Yesterday did you not soar in pride over your peo-
> ple,
>> oh my Khan?
> But today, as one dead, a rumbling chariot bears you
> onward,
>> oh my Khan!
> Have you really abandoned your wife and your chil-
> dren,
>> oh my Khan?
> Have you left all your faithful subjects?
> Yesterday, did you not wheel in the sky like a falcon,
>> oh my Khan?
> And today, as an unbroken colt after a wild gallop,
>> have you not stumbled and fallen,
>> oh my Khan?
> Or as the new grown grass been uprooted by the
>> tempest?
> After barely sixty years, and at the very moment
>> when you were about to give the nine banners the
>> joy of repose, have you not been taken from them
>> and remain cast down?

Some historians say that to keep the death of Genghis
Khan a secret, all persons encountered by the procession
as it moved northward were slain. An equal number of

historians say this is not true, that even the Mongols would not stoop to such barbaric practices at a time of great mourning.

The death of Genghis Khan was not admitted publicly until his body was carried to his home camp on the Kerulen River. He was buried on the western slopes of the Khingan Mountains. But, as of today, the Mongol emperor's grave has not been located.

FIFTEEN

MAN OF MANY SIDES

GENGHIS Khan's genius as a military leader is unquestioned. He was, perhaps, the greatest commander in all history. He was more than that, however. He was a man who not only conquered a vast territory—half of the world—but was able to keep it under his strong control, although his empire stretched over four thousand miles from east to west, from the Sea of Japan to deep into Russia.

He was a man who demanded absolute loyalty and gave loyalty in return. He must have been capable of outstanding character judgment. Time and again he turned a conquered enemy into a loyal follower. He placed great trust in these converts and nowhere is it recorded that any of them betrayed him.

Genghis Khan was strong-willed, but he was not a dictator; he did not refuse to accept any questioning of his decisions. He listened to advice in his councils and took it.

114

He was superstitious, but in the age in which he lived, the sayings of soothsayers were followed all over the civilized world. Before his departure from the Altai Mountains late in July, 1219, a heavy snow storm spread two feet of snow over his camp. This most unusual happening for that time of year puzzled and worried the Mongol emperor. He sought an interpretation from one of his soothsayers. The soothsayer said the snowfall was an omen, predicting victory for the emperor of the northern climes over the emperor of the southern. Genghis Khan did conquer the emperor of the southern climes, the Khwarazm Shah. It is no wonder that the victor placed great faith in the interpretations of his soothsayers.

Genghis Khan's admiration of bravery was displayed time and time again. It did not matter if the feat of bravery was demonstrated by friend or foe. During his conquest of the Khorezimian Empire, Prince Jalal ad-Din jumped his horse twenty feet into the surging Indus River in making his escape. Although displeased at the escape of the prince, Khan said, "Happy the father of such a son," and held up the act of bravery to his own sons.

Genghis Khan was also capable of forgiving his enemies. He demonstrated this in the many occasions when Tughrul, khan of the Keraits, betrayed him. He also was willing to restore Jamukha to his position as his sworn brother, and Jamukha had been his implacable enemy for years.

The cruelty of Genghis Khan and the atrocities perpetrated by his warriors play an important part in any biography of the Mongol leader. During his conquest of the Khorezimian Empire, when the inhabitants of a city killed the governor appointed by Prince Tului to rule them, one historian says that Genghis Khan ordered his Mongols to slay every one in the city, and one million six hundred thousand persons were massacred.

Although historians dispute the extent of barbaric slaughter by the Mongols, they do not question that on numerous occasions the Mongols did massacre all the inhabitants of a captured city. In general, these massacres took place when the hostile element in the captured city revolted against the Mongol garrison left behind to rule. Such rebellion brought swift retaliation on the part of the Mongols. They struck back, recapturing the city, exterminating all living things in it, and then burning the city to the ground. Sites of once proud cities became grazing grounds for cattle. This ruthless slaughter served yet another Mongol purpose—the intimidation of other towns and cities on the Mongols' road to conquest.

In his destruction of many centers of civilization, the shrewd Genghis Khan spared the highly skilled workmen, the artists and artisans, and the more learned scholars. These people were forced to serve the Mongols and, in time, many of them became loyal followers of the leader and of his lieutenants, who ruled the provinces of his widespread empire.

116

Genghis Khan was as remarkable a statesman as he was a general. A conquered province would be placed under the rule of a relative or a trusted lieutenant. The Khan insisted that there be no feuding or warfare among adjacent provinces. He was kept well informed about his entire empire, far-flung though it was, by his systems of yams, fast-riding couriers who could cover two hundred miles a day. An endless flow of information traveled daily between the rulers of the provinces and Genghis Khan's headquarters, even when he was on the march. That he was able to maintain a firm hand over provinces thousands of miles away is a tribute to the Mongol conqueror's ability to inspire loyalty, as well as to the close contact he maintained with his lieutenants.

The yam system served another important purpose. It opened up trade routes between Asia and the civilized nations of Eastern Europe. Before Genghis Khan brought Asia under his control, trading caravans ventured into the mysterious East with fear as their constant companion. Bandits struck often and ruthlessly. But Genghis insisted that all communication routes be kept open, not only for his couriers but for the movement of nomadic tribes and for traders. Any molestation of trading caravans brought instant reprisal. The bandits were quickly rounded up and executed.

The strong ruling hand of Genghis Khan and his descendants was felt in conquered countries for scores of years after his death.

In Iran and Transoxiana the rule of the Khans was not replaced until 1370, nearly a century and a half after Genghis Khan's death.

The great Mongol empire did not collapse with the death of its founder. Genghis Khan's sons carried on, and his grandson Kublai extended the empire hewed out by his grandfather to even greater domains. It is Kublai who is recognized as the founder of the Mongol dynasty in China, although it was his grandfather who made the dynasty possible.

Historians have such conflicting views on almost all phases of Genghis Khan's life that no true, clear picture of the Mongol leader comes through. But all are in agreement that Genghis Khan was, indeed, one of the greatest conquerors of all time.

Index

119